A Lincolnshire Lad Looks Back
Nocton Estate - The Home of Smith's Crisps

First Published 2003

ISBN 0-9540222-9-7

A catalogue record for this book is available from the British Library

Published by
Japonica Press
Low Green Farm, Hutton, Driffield,
East Yorkshire, YO25 9PX
United Kingdom

Book layout by Banks Design

About the author

Len's father was born at West Burton near Gainsborough, Lincolnshire in 1907. His parents were in farming all their lives. From West Burton they moved to Bishop Norton and then to Bardney Dairies where they lived at Tile House Beck. The house is still there today. Len's father moved to Partridge Farm in Nocton Fen, Lincoloshire in 1925 as second chap to George Reeve. J.H. Dennis owned the Estate at this time, until 1936 when Smith's Potato Crisps bought it.

Len's mothers parents came from a small village near Chester, called Neston. They moved to live in a farm Cottage at Waddingworth, near Horncastle, where his mother was born. They then moved to Bardney Dairies where his mother spent her early days. She was sent out to service at Bardney Manor, which belonged to Alderman Sumner. She met Len's father in the early 30's and they married in 1932 and settled down to married life at Todd's Farm, Nocton Fen where Len's father had been promoted to head Waggoner. This is where Len was born on 13th July 1937, the third of five children: Nellie, Brian, Len, Dennis and Mavis.

Len spent his life in the parish of Nocton, apart from a short spell in Potterhanworth Fen, which was still part of the estate. The Nocton estate was to be his life.

Len started work on the Estate in July 1952, as soon as he left school, he worked there until 1997, a period of 45 years. He found his wife Pauline at Kirkstead near Woodhall Spa in 1958 and they were married at Horncastle in Dec 1960. They have two children: Nigel and Diane and four grandchildren: Tom, Joe, Lauren & Jessica.

Len has seen many changes during his lifetime and not all to the good. In the early days there were horses, traction engines and the light railway system which were eventually replaced by the tractors and lorries. Each time any of these were replaced it was always with ones larger and soon fewer.

Houses got better with the coming of piped water and in some cases electricity and some houses were even fitted with baths.

Due to redundancy, Len retired early and now lives in Metheringham.

Introduction

This book is a personal account of my life in and around Nocton, and includes some of my family history.

I was born in the depths of the Nocton Fen in 1937 – a real Lincolnshire Yellow Belly! I spent most of my school days at Nocton. When I left school I got a job in farming on the Nocton Estate, which at that time was owned by Smith's Potato Crisps.

In these pages you will find stories of what was happening in the Fen during the war years, changes on the farm and in the village, all the way through my 45 years of working on the Nocton Estate. There are pictures of working scenes on the estate, from the days of horse-drawn implements to the mechanised equipment that is used today. There are also snippets about my family and social life in Nocton Village.

I would like to add that, as a sufferer from Parkinson's disease, I have found that my computer has opened up new horizons for me, and enabled me to produce this book. I would encourage anyone in a similar situation to explore the endless possibilities a computer can offer.

How the Crisps Name Came to Nocton

Frank Smith, who was the founder of Smith's Potato Crisps, came to Lincolnshire looking for prime potato growing land. He had started producing crisps in 1929, and his business was so successful that he decided he needed a farming company that could grow enough good quality potatoes to supply his company. In 1936 he bought the Nocton Estate of some 8,000 acres. The farm was well equipped for this enterprise: it was one of the largest in Britain; and it had a light railway system covering the whole area, which was used to move produce around the estate.

After buying the estate in 1936 it became apparent to that a local crisp factory would be an advantage, so in 1938 Frank Smith opened a new factory on Newark Road, Lincoln. The potatoes were lifted and graded in the field and put into 1cwt bags, then loaded onto the light railway and moved to the main headquarters at Nocton and Dunston station. They were then transferred to lorries or to British Rail trains to be taken to the crisp factories.

At the factory the potatoes were

unloaded by hand, washed by women factory workers and to fed into a slicer. The women would fry the slices in pure nut oil, then the crisps were put into packets or tins with a small portion of salt twisted in a piece of blue paper. They sold in shops and cafæs for 2d and 1d for the packets, and 6d for a tin.

Smith's Potato Crisps was taken over by General Mills of America in 1967, but operations carried on as before. Then in 1975 General Mills decided to sell off the Smith's Food Group, as it become known. The Guardian Royal Insurance Group, which had formed a farming company in the name of British Field Products, then bought the estate – they were already farming land in South Lincolnshire, Cambridgeshire and Norfolk.

The estate at Nocton was made up of around 5,500 acres of fen land, being about 10 ft above sea level; the remaining 2,500 acres being mainly heathland. There were about 1,000 scotch half-bred breeding ewes. The crop rotation was a six-year rotation of wheat – potatoes – wheat – peas – wheat and then sugar beet. 3,000 acres of wheat was grown annually along with 500 acres of Spring barley, 1,000 acres of peas, 1,000 acres of beet and 400 acres of potatoes. Yields of wheat were around 44 cwt per acre; spring barley 35cwt; sugar beet about 14 to 15 tons per acre; and 12 to 14 tons of potatoes were produced per acre.

At this time the farm general manager was Mr Jim Smart, and the arable manager was Mr Rod Hargreaves. There were 85 staff, 60 of these worked on the arable side of the farm. Nocton Hall was still a Royal Air Force Hospital (it finally closed in March 1983, having been used as a hospital since 1947). Most of the cottages in the villages of Nocton and Dunston were also owned by the estate: there were about 100 at this time, 30 of which were occupied by retired staff, who were permitted to live there for the rest of their lives rent and rates free.

Mr Frank Smith, Founder of Smith's Potato Crisps

Grandad Crawford

Charles Leonard Crawford was born in the Stickney area of Boston. He lost his parents at the age of 8 years, and moved to Aljarkirk to live with his uncle who kept the Case Is Altered Inn. His name was Frederick Joseph Hanks. He was born in 1830, and took over as licensee of the Inn from his father, Robert Hanks, in 1855.

Robert Hanks had been the licensee for twenty years, and prior to the Case Is Altered being built he had kept the Cross Keys Inn at Sutterton for twenty five years. He also rented from the Government the toll bridge over the River Welland known as Fosdyke Bridge, and another bridge spanning the river at the entrance into Boston from Kirton.

The annual cost was £1,100.

He was a remarkable character, measuring three feet across the shoulders. He always wore silver-buckled shoes, blue silk stockings with one garter of deep blue on the left leg, light blue velvet knee breeches with coat and vest the same, and a cravat more usual to the decade previous to his time, finishing off with the silk top hat of the early 17th century. (These clothes are still held by the family as an heirloom.)

Robert married four times: three of his wives already had families, being widows, so he had four wives and seven different families.

He came to a tragic end, being drowned one very dark night by falling from the Fosdyke Bridge, on 24th November 1858.

Frederick Joseph Hanks was the only child of Robert's first wife, so he became heir to the Case Is Altered Inn, plus a row of houses with land attached. Frederick was highly respected throughout the dis-

trict, and was a great friend to many of the working class. He was also father to 21 children, all by the same mother!

He was for many years overseer of Algakirk, and for the early period of these years he was Constable of the Parish. He was a familiar figure for many miles around.

After living with the Frederick Hanks and his family for a while my Grandad ran away. For a short time he worked on a beer dray in Ruskington. He then moved to Cheshire, where he helped to dig the Manchester-Sheffield water main, and it was there at Neston, near Chester, that he met my Granny, Martha Ann Newton. They were married at Wallasey church.

They moved back to Lincolnshire to live with an uncle at Waddingworth, where they had five of their nine children. Then, when my mother Nellie was born in 1909, they had to move as the house had become too small for the growing family. Grandad went to work for R C Viner at Greenbank Farm, Minting Wood, and then moved on to Bardney Dairies where he worked as a labourer for John Needham. The children had to walk to Bardney school and back each day – a round trip of seven miles.

The farm was eventually sold to a Mr Poucher.

My Grandad then moved to Tattersal, to work for Mr Tom Smithson, from there to Kirkby on Bain, and then to Tumby Woodside to work for a Mr Trafford. He retired in 1947 and moved to Youngwood near Bardney, were he spent the final eleven years of his life before he died, aged 77. My granny died at the age of 75.

During his retirement at Youngwood,

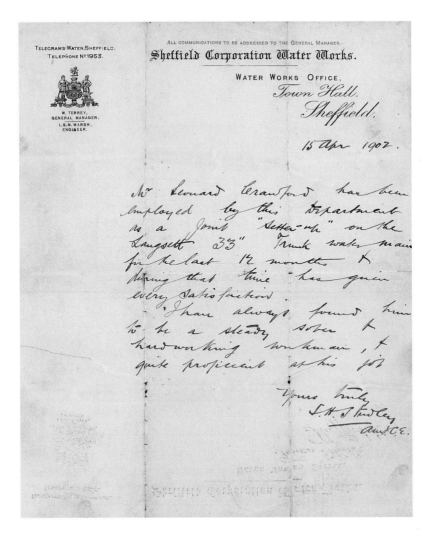

Grandad still worked for local farmers at harvest time. One of these farmers was a Mr Pepper of Kingthorpe: I remember Grandad used to go to work and back using Mr Pepper's pony and trap for transport.

SHEFFIELD CORPORATION WATER WORKS

15th April 1902

Mr Leonard Crawford has been employed by this department as a Joint "setter up" on the Lansett 33" Trunk water main for the last 12 months, and during that time has given every satisfaction.

I have always found him to be a steady sober and hardworking workman, and quite proficient at his job.

Yours truly

S H Studley

Snippets of Family History

On my Dad's side I know very little, as I cannot remember Grandad and Granny Woodhead - I just remember my father talking about Sturton by Stow, Kexby and Bishop Norton. When the family moved to this area they lived and worked at Bardney Grange, then at Tile House, Stainfield.

My Dad came to Nocton Fen in 1925 when he was 18 years old. He came to lodge at Partridge Farm as 'second chap' to George Reeve. (George was later successful in setting up a haulage business at Bardney).

At Partridge Farm there were eight horses. George worked and looked after four and Dad the other four. It was a seven-day-a-week job, each day starting at 5:30 am to enable the horses to be fetched in from the paddock in summer or the crewyard in winter. The horses were then fed and prepared for work at 6:30. On Sundays work was restricted to feeding and stable work only, unless it was harvest time.

The work in the fields started at 6:30 am, with a 30 minute break at 11.00 am, and then work continued until 2:30 pm (called loasing time), when the horses were brought back home, groomed and fed, stables cleaned, and crew yards bedded with clean straw. The waggoner would then go in for his dinner; back to work by 5:30 to feed the horses and either take them to the paddock in summer or turn them into the crewyard in winter. In the winter months when they were in the crewyard they were given some supper at 9:00 pm.

On Mum's side of the family (the Crawfords); Mum used to talk about living at Bardney Dairies, and remembered the long walk to and from the Wesleyan school each day at Bardney.

An example of one of my Grandad's contracts of employment:

On Behalf of R C Viner Esq

I hereby agree to hire C L Crawford as Waggoner upon a farm in the Parish of Minting from Ladyday 1909 to Ladyday 1910 on the following conditions, to have 13/6d per week in money. 30 Stone Pork. 40 Peck of Potatoes. 13 Gallons of beer. 60 Faggots. 10/- for stable lights. House and Garden rent free. Two weeks pay for illness. If any dispute should arise one month's notice should be given on either side.

Signed by Willam Lunn

April 6th 1909

Descendants of Crawford

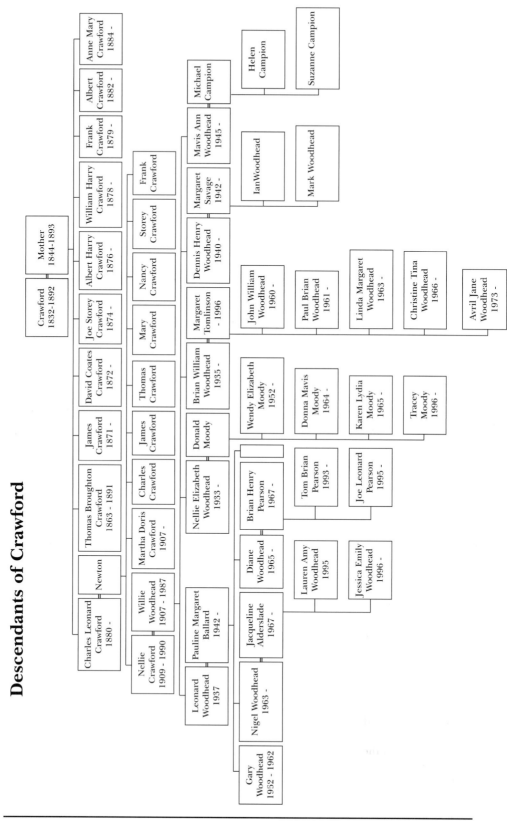

Nocton in 1872

The following is a description of Nocton and the surrounding area as it was in 1872.

'Nocton is a well-built and pleasant village in a gently undulating, well wooded area near the head of a small rivulet between Lincoln Heath and the Cardyke Navigation, 7 miles south-east of Lincoln and 5 miles south-west of Bardney railway station. The parish has 518 inhabitants and 5340 acres of land, extending 4 miles westward over the now-fertile Heath, nearly to Dunston Pillar, and 5 miles eastward across the Fens to the river Witham. An act for improving the drainage of Nocton, Potterhanworth, and Branston Fens was obtained in 1831. Since then steam pumping engines have been erected at various places in the above parishes on the side of the Witham. The quantity of fen and marsh land in Nocton Parish liable for the drainage tax is 2315 acres, 1 rood 17 perches. There are 200 acres of woodland in the parish. The Marquis of Ripon is Lord of the Manor and owner of the soil except the Glebe.

Nocton Hall, the pleasant seat of the Marquis of Ripon situated in an extensive wooded park, is a large and elegant structure in the Elizabethan style. It was erected in 1841 on the site of the previous manor house, which was burnt down in 1834.

About half a mile away is Nocton Priory, founded in the reign of Steven by Robert d'Archy, for black canons of the Augustine order. At the dissolution, it was valued at £57.19s.2d. and had 5 monks.

The site was granted to Charles, Duke of Suffolk, but in the reign of Elizabeth it passed to Sir Henry Stanley, who converted the Priory into a residence. This was demolished and replaced by a mansion by Sir William Ellys, in the latter part of the 17th Century. At this time the grounds were planted and laid out in the prevailing syle of the times, but they were much improved by the Earl of Buckinghamshire, the subsequent owner. The prospects are varied and extensive, and near the house stands one of the finest chestnut trees in England.

The present owner, the Most Hon. George Frederick Samuel Robinson, K.G., P.C. D.C.L. was created Marquis of Ripon in 1871. He was born on October 4th, 1827. He succeeded his father as third Earl of Ripon in January 1859, and his uncle as third Earl de Grey in November of the same year. His son Frederick Oliver, Earl de Grey, was born in 1852.

The vicarage, valued at £575, is in the gift of the Marquis of Ripon, and incumbency of the Rev. Edward Wilson, MA, Prebendary of Lincoln, who has a good modern vicarage house. The tithes were commuted for allotments, containing 341 acres 2 roods, at the enclosure. The poor parishioners have the interest of £50 left by Sir Richard Ellys in 1740, of £10 given by Sir Francis Dashwood, and of £100, left by the earl of Buckinghamshire, Sir Richard Ellys, and Sir J Dashwood.

The Marquis of Ripon supports a school, and there are in the Village four cottages (known as Ripon Row) for the free use of poor families. In the church are several monuments, one to the only daughter of the late Earl of Ripon, one in memory of the late Vicar, and one in memory of the late Earl of Buckinghamshire, father of the Countess of Ripon.'

A Lincolnshire Lad Looks Back

Nocton Estate - The Home ofSmith's Crisps

TD8 is a field down Nocton Fen, like many other fields, where houses once stood. In the north west corner of this field stood two three-bedroom farm cottages. It was in one of these cottages, on the 13th July, 1937 that I was born.

My father was a waggoner looking after and working four heavy horses: Captain, Bonnie, Star and Daisy. My mother had a full-time job looking after the house and myself, my elder brother and sister.

Births in those days were a do-it-your-self sort of job. Nanna Sewel, who lived a field away in another farm cottage, was soon notified and was there on such occa-

was used to carry drinking water for all the farm cottages. There were 28 occupied farm cottages on the Nocton Fen and Potterhanworth Fen parts of the estate, at that time. As well as the water, all of the feed, for horses, pigs and bullocks that were kept in most farm crewyards, was carried by the railway.

Drinking water was discharged from the railway into metal tanks that were sited close to the railside. The tanks were topped up each week. The tank lids would most likely be a sheet of corrugated zinc or similar.

Mother used to have to carry all the

Roy Sewell Loco driver prepares to haul a load of potatoes to the main railhead

sions to do the necessary until someone could bike the three miles to Bardney to get the doctor. His transport was also a bike. I later had another brother and sister.

Farm roads were cart tracks with ruts that were made by the horses and carts. These would be full of water in the winter and dry and bumpy in the summer.

Almost all the farms were linked by the Nocton Estate Light Railway system. This

water from this tank, by bucket, to the house for washing, cooking, cleaning and so on.

The house had an open fireplace in all rooms. We had no electricity, only paraffin lamps, and candles and a black iron cooking range in the living room. This had an oven on one side and an open top boiler on the other. We used a long handled ladle to fill the boiler and also to take water out. Each time you took out a ladleful you had to put one back. If you let the boiler get empty it would boil dry and could crack.

We had a little outhouse with a large copper used on washdays, which were mostly Mondays, it was also used for boiling pig potatoes and food scraps as most workers kept at least one pig to be reared and fattened ready for killing for bacon in the winter.

My dad used to fetch the house coal from Bardney railway station, one ton at a time, by horse and cart. It cost about five shillings per ton and he had to weigh the empty cart at Bardney Sugar factory on the way there and then weigh it again when loaded. This cost him sixpence.

The toilet was situated halfway down the garden at the back of the house. It was a three seater, for two adults and one child, so if you were frightened to go in the dark at night, you could take another member of the family with you. It was a cistern toilet like a hole in the ground. When it was full, my dad had to dig a deep hole down the garden by using a with bucket on a rope he would empty it. It would probably need emptying once a year.

The garden was quite large. We had to grow all our own vegetables because the nearest shops were at Bardney and that was a bicycle ride away.

A Mr Dawson used to come down the fen once a week with his grocery cart from the Bardney Co-op. Mum used to have an order book so when he brought the order one week she would fill her order in for him to bring next time he came. The Co-op milkman used to come every day but he couldn't get down the roads so everyone who wanted milk had a milk box at the end of the track to leave the milk checks in. Someone then had to walk down the track each day to fetch the milk home.

I think I was about eight years old when my dad bought our first radio set, of course with no electricity it had to have an accumulator, which was like a small car battery. They were a good thing but of course they gradually lost the power and went flat. This would mostly occur when we were listening to *Dick Barton Special Agent* or *Journey Into Space*. When this happened the accumulator had to be taken to George Hensons Bike shop at Bardney to be recharged. This would take about a day, so you would bike to Bardney one day to take it and bike back again the next to fetch it back. It used to cost 8d (3p). Eventually dad bought a second accumulator so we could plan it that we always had one to use while the other was being recharged. Later we learned that a double cell-battery from our bike lamps could be used, and also when they lost their power we could put them in the oven a few times and this would partly charge them up.

When I was three, Britain was at war and soon after ration books were issued: coupons for sweets, coupons for clothes, coupons for almost everything.

1942-43 CLOTHING BOOK

This book may not be used until the holder's name, full postal address and National Registration (Identity Card) Number have been plainly written below IN INK.

NAME (BLOCK LETTERS) _WILLIE WOODHEAD._

ADDRESS (BLOCK LETTERS) _NOCTON FEN. SOUTHREY._

(TOWN) _LINCOLN._ (COUNTY) _LINCS_

NATIONAL REGISTRATION (IDENTITY CARD) NUMBER
TJDB . /132 / 1

Read the instructions within carefully, and take great care not to lose this book

Page 1

The author with the Lancaster propeller, Potterhanworth Fen, 1986

I can't remember a lot about the war years apart from the noise of Lancaster Bombers taking off from Bardney and other local airfields. I remember one Saturday morning my dad was ploughing out sugar beet with a pair of his horses in TD6, which was a field about 500 yards or so from the house. I had taken dad a pot of tea, as he stopped for lunch about 9am, when we heard the moan of a German fighter. It was flying very low over the banks of the delf. Just short of where the delf joins the River Witham stood the steam pumping station, which had a tall chimney. As the fighter got near, it started to fire at the chimney then it turned, south following the Witham to Boston and out to sea.

Another memory from the war was that, on 1st October 1943, my dad was carting potatoes from a gang of women who were picking potatoes in what was called the Washway. This was low land running alongside the River Witham, myself and my pal Nipper, whose Mum was in the picking gang, were going along the track to the field, when we heard a loud noise.

Turning west to look, we saw, coming over Nocton Wood, a Halifax Bomber (probably Halifax S DC275) in trouble. It was heading straight towards the potato field and rotating like a windmill. It just missed the potato gang and crashed over the ditch in the next field. Later we were told it was from RAF Swinderby and had a crew of nine who were all killed in the crash.

In July 1943, a Lancaster Bomber from no. 9 Squadron at Bardney (probably ED489 or ED656) took off for a test run after some repairs. Just after getting airborne over Southrey Wood, the crew started to bale out as the engines had problems. Close to the Bardney Causeway, the bomber exploded and crashed in a potato field (PF1). Even now, 50 years after, you can still find pieces as you cultivate the field. You can also see the repair joint in the overhead electric cables that were broken in the crash. In 1986, when Richmonds Drainage was working in the field, they dug up a propeller and part of an engine, these are now at the East Kirkby Air Museum.

Other crashes in the fen included a Wellington Bomber (No X9872), on 10 September 1942, that crashed into farm buildngs down the bottom of Dunston Fen. This plane was from RAF Finningley. It destroyed the farm buildings and the crew of six were killed. A Sterling Bomber crashed halfway down Dunston Fen. A Defiant (N 3333 Mk1), from 255 Squadron at Kirton Lindsey, crashed at Lark Farm, Nocton Fen on 4 May 1941. Two crew escaped safely. Then there was a Beaufighter 11F (R2475), from 409 Squadron, that crashed on Plough Hill at Potterhanworth Booths, just past The Plough public house, on 19 January 1942.

We had a searchlight battery ststioned on the Abbey Hill at Wasp's Nest.

Owing to having many airfields nearby, we also had a dummy airfield at Partridge Farm which consisted of reflectors and lights across (P7]. These were switched on to attract enemy aircraft when they were in the area. This kept them away from the important bomber bases, scattered around us.

Another vague memory of wartime was late one evening, maybe a year or so later, the sky was filled with aircraft heading south, quite a lot were towing gliders.

road ends, and quite a lot at Wasp's Nest. There would be at least 50 on board by the time we arrived at Nocton School. The bus was either a Commer or a Bedford 29 seater.

Children went to Nocton between the ages of 5 and 15. (This was to change in 1950].

It was a smashing school. Miss Turner was infant school teacher, Miss Nichols teacher in the second class, and the head-master was Mr Emerson, who also taught

Nocton School, 1950

There seemed to be hundreds and the noise was deafening.

School Days

I started school when I was five years old. We had to go to Nocton School, as this was the nearest North Kesteven School for us. Gus Parker's bus used to start picking up children near Bardney bridge and come right through the Fen. There would be children to pick up at most of the farm

the top class He was a very nice chap, but very strict. He had a cane but very seldom needed to use it.

At school playtimes we played football, quick cricket, rounders, tiggey and season-al games such as conkers, whip and top, and marbles. The girls would play hop-scotch, skipping, ring-a-ring o' roses and join us playing rounders.

Nocton Hall grounds had several orchards, one of the best ones was owned by a Mr Clark. In the summertime he would fill his barrow with fallen apples and bring them to school at playtime. He would get all the children standing in a row, and he would throw the apples for us kids to run for. He called it an apple scramble.

We were given a third of a pint of milk per day, at school. We also had a nice hot dinner but this cost us 7d (3 new pence].

Mr & Mrs Ash kept the Nocton Post Office, we used to go there and buy a 1d packet of broken crisps.

During the war years the American Military had the main part of the Hall grounds. Whenever an American met any of us children, we would be given chewing gum and lifesavers (fruit sweets].

My Younger Years

My Dad used to keep a ferret so we often went out with him to get us a cheap dinner. We also had a mongrel dog, which would catch many a rabbit. The dog also protected us kids. I remember one afternoon Mr Quibbel, who lived next door, was chasing us kids around the farmyard with the clothes prop in his hands. As soon as our dog Rover saw this, he had him by the trousers. That put an end to that game.

As soon as we were old enough, about eight or nine, we used to get a stick and in harvest time, when we were on school holidays, we would spend almost all of our time in the fields, with the binders, catching rabbits. Sometimes we saw a fox come out just before the binders finished the field. Most times, when that happened, there would be no live rabbits in the crop,

The McCormick Deering Binder at work

only dead rabbits, pheasants, and partridges, mostly with their heads bitten off.

Very often there would be a gang of six men following the binders and stooking the sheaves. Us kids would often run a rabbit round and round until the rabbit and we were tired out. Then, very often, one of the men stooking would step in and he had himself a nice dinner.

Mostly where pigs or cattle were kept or when there were corn stacks in the farmyards you would have quite a lot of rats around, so you could take old Rover and spend a few hours at night catching rats. During the winter months the steam traction engine and threshing machine would come along with a gang of 12 men and thresh the corn stacks that were in the stackyard. This was a happy time for old Rover. He would spend all day with them and there wouldn't be many rats and mice that escaped. At one time I remember, if

Left to Right: F. Robinson, A. Saundby, B. Etheridge, J. Robinson, Irishman, D. Wass, J. Vickers, D. Wass, W. Hubbard, E. Dickinson, H. Franklin, B. Watson on wheel, Steam threshing Nocton, 1946

we nipped the tail end off every rat we caught and kept it, the government would pay 2d each for them.

Steam Threshing

A 12 man threshing gang consisted of an engine and drum man, two men bagging and carrying corn, two men on the corn stack handing the sheaves up onto the threshing drum. On the drum would be a man cutting the strings and a man feeding them into the threshing drum, there would be one person in the chaff hole. They would have to carry the chaff clear of the farmyard for burning. If wheat was being threshed then it was sometimes bagged up to be fed to the horses. There would be one person in the pulse (short straw) hole. This was mostly carried away and burnt. Then there would be two men on the straw stack, and another carrying water for the steam engine.

Wheat was put into 18 stone bags (about 112kg); barley into 16 stone(100kg) and oats into 12 stone (75kg). The corn would be weighed and then, after tying up the mouth of the bag, it would be wound up on what we called a winding barrow to the height of the man's shoulders. He would get it across his shoulders and carry it up a plank into a box waggon on the light railway system. When the waggon was full, a ticket would be made out giving details of variety, number of field and so on. At around 3 o'clock in the afternoon, a loco (small engine or train) would come along and collect any full waggons and leave empty ones in their places. Off it would go. Each train could pull six full waggons, (18 ton). When they arrived at Wasp's Nest, two engines were needed to pull the six waggons up the Abbey hill. After getting up the hill they then proceeded to the railhead at Nocton and Dunston station which was the estate headquarters.

Sometimes a waggoner would come in an afternoon for a load of chaff to take back to his stable. There was quite a bit of competition between the waggoners to see who could have the best set of horses. An extra bag or two of corn now and again would make their coats shine. When the waggoner came for some chaff, depending on who was in the corn department, he could probably hide a bag or two of corn amongst his bags of chaff.

One particular tale was that, one day, two waggoners came for a load of chaff each and managed to get a bag or two of corn. In doing so, one man didn't hide them both in his load, one bag of corn was put on the back of the load. When he headed for home, he was the first waggon, he hadn't got far up the Nocton fen road (heading for Wasp's Nest) when the horse pulling the second waggon got a smell of the bag on the front waggon, he decided to have a nag at it. He managed to eat some but more was being spilt on the road. Then in the late afternoon when the Estate Manager came riding down the Abbey hill on his horse, there were crows along the full length of the fen road from Decoy Farm to Wasp Nest stables. It didn't need a detective to find who was responsible. The waggoner was politely told not to do it again and he had to take any other bags back to the threshing gang in his own time.

In the summer months the horses were

A. Page and L. Overton

put out to grass at nights and weekends. Dad used to take them out about 4.30 in the afternoon and fetch them back at 5 o'clock in the morning.

The land adjoining the River Witham was like a marsh so it was all rough grass, its only use at that time was for grazing it (this area of land was called the Washway].

The Nocton Delf was nice and clean at that time. If we got bad weather in the winter and the water train could not get through, Mum used to carry water from the Delf for cooking and drinking.

Us kids used to get one of Dad's kidney bean sticks, Mum's button thread and a bent knob pin and off we used to go to the steam pumping engine where Mr Lovely had a little rowing boat he would let us use. The water was so clear we could see the perch swimming under the boat. With a nice red worm dangled in front of them, we could be pulling fish out all day. We used to go home saying we had caught no end of fish but what we had been doing was pulling the same few fish out and dropping them back in to catch again.

Our yearly outings used to be Bardney Fair in August, a Sunday School outing to Skegness and a trip on the steam train from Bardney to Tumby Woodside to see my granny and grandad.

I remember once when I was about seven Mr Flintham, who was Farm Foreman at Bridge Farm, bought a car. I think it was the first one in Nocton Fen. One of his lads was called John and he was about nine, he asked Dad if I could go to Skegness with them to be a pal for John. I was able to go with them on the Sunday. That trip was the highlight of my year.

On a winter's night, we would sit by the fire and help Mum cut up our old clothes into small strips then take turns with the snipper to make rugs for the house.

We, and other families living on the farms at the bottom of the Fen, were in the Southery postal district, which was on the other side of the river. The only way to get over the river to us was by using the ferry at the White Horse Inn. Eddy East was our postman at that time. He also used to come and measure the thatch that the men had put on the corn stacks because the thatchers were paid by the square yard.

We had a village hall at Wasp's Nest where Sunday School was held. We used to have one or two garden fetes each year. I remember Dad winning a pig once, and he also won a bantam cockerel. I remember the cockerel very well as when it was let loose with our other poultry in the farmyard, we soon found out why it had been given as a prize. Each time any of us kids went out in the yard, the cockerel used to chase us and jump at our legs. He had some big spurs on his legs. However, Mum soon put a stop to him: she had him upside down on a meat dish with some gravy round him.

The WI used to meet about once per month, we also had a dance each month.

Mr Crooks, who used to drive buses for Gus Parker, would start from Bardney with the three-piece band in the back of the bus. In the summer season there would be at least 40 Irishmen lodging in the fen. Quite a few of them would be picked up at the farm road ends along with some of the families.

Part of the hall had a drinks licence so adults could have a pint or two. Darts and dominoes were played. With the workers getting fewer in the fens, the village hall closed in 1958.

The Nocton Estate was divided into six sections, the three Nocton Fen sections had about 900 acres each: A, B, and C. Mr Redshaw was foreman on Section A, Mr Flintham on Section B and Mr Willoughby on Section C.

I cannot remember many tractors in the 1940s. The main work was still done by the horses, about 60 in the fen at that time. There was a couple of Caterpillar D4s, a couple of Caterpillar 22s and maybe the odd yellow Ford, towards the end of the 1940s. There were at least two

Nocton Fen Social Club, 1947 closed in 1959

The only crawler tractor Mr J. Iverson could buy in 1946, a second hand Caterpillar D7 75hp

Leading and threshing at Nocton 1940s

Mr and Mrs Fred Hewitt gapping beet

sets of steam engines on the estate. These used to do most of the cultivations at that time.

A cultivating team consisted of about seven men, two engine drivers, two stokers, a man to steer the plough or drag, a waggoner to cart the water and coal to the steam engines and also a full time cook. One of the drivers had to get up very early in the morning to go to the engines to stoke them up so they had plenty of steam up for when the rest of the gang came to work.

The men who worked in the fen came from Nocton, Dunston, Metheringham, Potterhanworth, Bardney and Southery. The men from Southery had to come over the Witham by the ferry at the bottom of Dunston Fen. Almost all the men would come on bikes, there were a few that walked. There were about 15 to 20 men on each section, plus about 12 Irishmen in the summer season. During the war, instead of the Irishmen, Len Scott would bring a lorry load of German POWs, from Wellingore and Potterhanworth, to help pick the potatoes.

When I was about nine years old my dad bought me a bicycle, this was very handy in the fen, it enabled me to go shopping to Bardney for my mum (mostly Saturday mornings). Mum used to write out separate orders for each shop so all I had to do was go to the certain shop and hand the paper and ration book over to the person there. They would check if I had enough coupons and then give me my order. At Bardney, there was Brackenbury the chemist, Gus Parker the butcher, Harry Dawson had a boot and shoe shop (he was also a bookie). Next door was Blades sweet shop, on the Angel corner was George Hensons bike shop, opposite was Holmes and Burrows drapers. Just along Station Road was Saddler Cooke, opposite was Thomsons tobacco shop, a little further on was the bakery of M E Clift, they also had a grocery shop next door. A little further down the road, was Blithes newsagents, next door was the barbers shop, opposite that was Gus Parker's bus depot and garage, a little further down was Quincey & Holdens grocery shop.

Down at the bottom of Station Road, opposite Morells Cannery, was Taylors sweet shop. If you had the pocket money you could buy certain sweets without coupons. Also down the bottom of Station Road was J W Clifts bakehouse and opposite that was the Quincey Brothers' garage. There was Hanningtons small sweet and grocery shop in Queen Street and Harsley & Knowls had the fish shop. The pubs were The Black Horse on Wragby Road, the Angel Hotel at the top of Station Road and the Nags Head opposite. Down the bottom of Station Road were the Jolly Sailor and the Railway Hotel, just over the bridge was the Sloop Inn and down the Witham bank was the The Anchor.

I could use my bike to go to Bardney pictures, which were held one night a week in the village hall. I had three Aunties living at Youngwood, which is just outside Bardney, close to the airfield, so I could bike to see them. We used to sit for hours in the bedroom windows watching the Lancaster Bombers of No. 9 Squadron taking off and landing.

Pigs and Poultry

Living out on a farm in the 1940s and 50s, most families kept at least one pig and some poultry, either hens for their eggs or cockerels for fattening for the table.

We lived in Nocton Fen and with Mum and Dad having five children, we used to keep two pigs for fattening up for our own use.

Dad would buy a couple of young pigs about six weeks old, during June or July. These would be fed on household waste and boiled potatoes. By late November or early December they would be getting somewhere near 25 stone in weight, My Dad would apply to the post office for a permit or licence to have one killed. As soon as the permit arrived, a butcher would be booked, mostly for a Sunday, as this would be Dad's only free day from work, although he would still have some stable work and horses to feed.

On the morning of the pig killing, Mum would be up first to get the copper full and the fire lit so as to have the water boiling by about 8 to 8-30 am. The butcher would come about 8 am. We had at least three butchers that we could use living nearby: Slim Jim Bellamy from Sotshole; Earn Gibson and Doug Storey from Bardney. As soon as the butcher arrived the pig would be caught. A rope would be put around his nose, and he would then be led to a gatepost or strong tree. There he would be tethered tightly by the rope. The butcher would cut the pig's throat using a long knife so that the blade would reach his heart. The pig would then bleed until it rolled over dead. A pig scratch (a two wheel flat trolley) was brought and the pig was loaded on the scratch. Scalding water was then brought from the copper and poured over the pig. This loosened the pig's whiskers, so the butcher, and anyone else that was able, could get a scraper and scrape off the whiskers. After the whiskers were removed the pig's toenails would be pulled off, next off with his head. Finally a slit would be made in each back leg to reveal a guider.

A camera, a stout length of oak wood especially made for this purpose, about a yard long was used. The rear legs were spread so as to put this piece of wood through the guider, then, with a set of pulleys, the pig would be hoisted up on the nearest tree or maybe in an open shed if the rafters were strong enough. Some families were lucky enough to own proper lifting poles.

With the pig hanging just clear of the ground, the belly could then be cut open and the intestines taken out. The butcher would empty the intestines so they could be scraped for sausage skins. When that was done he would take out the heart and lungs. The pig's bladder was often blown up and used as a football. Next the butcher would mark out the chines by cutting down each side of the spine and then chopping through the ribs.

The two strips of belly fat, or aprons, would be hung over the camera so as to cool and harden. These would be later rendered down for cooking lard and, when that was done you finished up with what we called scraps, which were hundreds of

small pieces of meat. These we could eat with bread. When the butcher had finished, the pig would then be pulled up a bit higher on the pulleys and left to cool and to set for the next four hours. The butcher would come back later and cut the pig up. Once the pig was killed and hung up to cure, the butcher was invited into the house for a large fried breakfast.

As soon as the butcher had gone there was plenty of work to be done: sausage skins to be scraped and washed; the heart could be cut into small pieces, ready to be added to the fries. The lungs or pluck, as they were called, could be cut up and put through the mincer, ready to be added to the minced meat. The pig's head could be brought in and cut into two pieces, the lower part could be cooked for a joint, and the top part, along with his ears, would be kept ready to be boiled down, with any other scraps, for brawn. The pastry could be made ready for the sausage rolls and pork pies. Salt could be spread out on the pantry floor ready to lay the meat in, to cure for bacon.

When the butcher returned in the afternoon, the pig would be lowered down on to the scratch, ready for him to start cutting up.

There would be the four trotters for the brawn, the spareribs to be used as soon as possible. These were not salted. Other parts were cut and carried into the pantry for covering with salt. There would be two hams, two shoulders, two flitches, and eight chines. The biggest chine nearest its head was rarely salted, it would mostly be stuffed with parsley for stuffed chine. It was often called the christening chine. It was very important to do the salting right. Any bloody areas around joints or bones, needed quite a lot of saltpetre to dry up the moisture. Every thing had to be rubbed well with the salt before it was finally laid in the pantry.The second pig would be killed about February.

When the pig was cured, it needed at least a month in salt, it would then be hung up in the kitchen. Most farm houses had large steel hooks in the ceiling for a couple of 30stone pigs.

The following week for Mum would be

very hectic. Several fries were made, and they would consist of bits of liver, kidney, heart, and some nice pieces of pork. One of these would be given to each friend and

One of two International Combine Harvesters at Nocton, 1950

International Baler at Nocton, 1950s

neighbour. Then the sausage meat would be made. Us children could help with this by turning the mincer to grind up the meat. Meat for the pork pies and mince meat was also prepared, the belly fat or aprons had to be cut up into small pieces and rendered down for lard, which would then be stored in large porcelain pans.

We were then committed to eating pork pies, sausages, fries, sparerib, sausage rolls, and brawn, or scraps until they were all cleaned up.

During the spring, Dad would buy about 20 young Aylesbury ducklings, about 30 white Sussex cockerels, and often six or eight young geese. These would be fed as well as possible to get them as fat as we could for Christmas. A day or two before

Fordson E27N and Massey Harris 701 Baler at Nocton, 1950s

Tractors on parade Nocton, 1946

The fine tractor fleet at Nocton, early 1946

LEFT: *Parade of tractors, 1946*

BELOW: *Ernie Turner proudly drives the old Fiat*

Xmas, we would start killing the poultry and every able bodied person would sit round the fire and pluck them until they were all finished. Mum would be busy drawing them, washing them and wrapping them up ready for us all to load on our bicycles to take to Bardney, where my father had a regular order for each bird. The goose and duck feathers were mostly washed and dried and made into cushions and featherbeds.

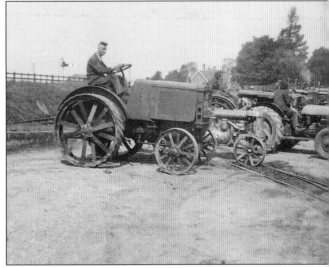

Moving House

The spring of 1947 was very severe: the dykes were all full to the top with snow; the fen roads were all

ABOVE: *Foxes Farm, 1950*

ABOVE:Our Loco driver Dick Dykes is on the right

ABOVE: Ben West, the Garthman

blocked and the light railway was snow-bound at Dunston Railhead.

In the spring of 1947 Mr Willoughby the Section C foreman put in his notice to retire.

The Estate Manager, Mr Robinson, came to see Dad and asked him if he would move across to the other side of the fen and take the foreman's job at Foxes Farm.

This was a very exciting time for us kids, as we were suffering with the winter weather. The snow was beginning to melt but with the thaw came the problems of flooding the cart tracks were full of water so this would give us problems flitting house. The only hope was if it kept on thawing then there would be a good chance that we could flit by light railway. By the first week in April, the snow was melting and the light railway was starting to move again, so it was decided that we could flit.

Dick Dykes, who was driver of the largest engine on the light railway, was organised to come to Toddies Farm, Nocton Fen for 9 o'clock in the morning. He arrived with two open trucks and two box waggons. With the wet and snowy conditions we had plenty of help from the farm men, carrying and loading the furniture and stuff. The two pigs had already been moved by horse and cart, but the poultry had to be caught and penned in one end of a box waggon. After everything was loaded there was still enough room to leave a side door open for us to sit and look out of, as we moved across the fens. We couldn't cut across the fen so we had to go down to the Wasps Nest to get the line to take us down the other side of

the fens and across to Foxes Farm. When we arrived at Foxes, some more men, who were to help us unload, met us. These were some of the staff that were to be under my dad's supervision on Section C. One man was Charlie Cox, he was head waggoner and also a lodger in the farmhouse. Another man was Ben West, the garthman, who was also a lodger.

One or two others were labourers that were about the farm at the time.

Foxes Farmhouse was a bigger house than the one we had left. Of course, with two lodgers (later to be three) we needed more room. There were five bedrooms, four up the main stairs (one of these was later made into a bathroom) the fifth bedroom was up another set of stairs. This was the largest bedroom and it was for the lodgers. Downstairs, we had two sitting rooms with open fires, the smaller of the two was to be used for my dad's office. We also had a long kitchen where we could all sit down for meals. At the sink end of the

Foxes Farmhouse, 1960s

kitchen, the ceiling was full of bacon hooks where we could hang two 30-stone pigs during the winter months. There was a large pantry, with a cold concrete floor, suitable for salting the pigs, to cure them for bacon.

Outside, across the causeway, was a large washhouse with a big copper for boiling the washing, boiling potatoes for the pigs and also for boiling the water for scalding the pig on pig killing days. Adjoining this was the cistern toilet which was emptied by hand about once a year. In the same block was a chicken house, big enough to hold about 50 chickens. With the hen house being next door to the toilet, they were both visited regularly by rats so we kept an air gun in the corner of the toilet and a torch. It was always a good idea to check to see if there were any rats, before you sat on the toilet.

The farm buildings consisted of stables for 16 horses with a partly covered crew-

Foxes Farm Crewyard with a hundred Hereford Bullocks, 1950s

yard for these, also four other crewyards big enough for 100 bullocks. There was a large barn for fertiliser storage, part of this was made into an Irishman's den for eight Irishmen in the summer season. There was another large barn for the garthman to mix his food for the bullocks. There were two open cart hovels, these could be used for some of the first tractors, before they had cabs on. Across the other side of

the stackyard was a large glasshouse suitable for holding 100 ton of seed potatoes, in boxes, during the winter. It was filled with tomatoes during the summer. We also had a large garden with 13 apple trees and three plum trees.

Foxes farmyard

New van at Nocton, 1950

Mr J. Ireson general manager, chats to Bill Redshaw on Fiat tractor, 1946

Another load reaches railhead

Potato Hoover at work, 1950s

there was a well that fed from a natural spring. There was a small water cart propped up near to the front of the house and someone would hitch a horse to it about once a week and go down to the well. It was about half a mile away, down towards Potterhanworth near Battles Fen Farm, when we got to the well, we could see it was a round brick walled structure about six feet across and six feet above ground. The well is still there today. When we arrived at the well we would open the lid. With the cart close to it, we had to climb on the top and, by using a bucket on a rope, we filled the cart with water, which would take quite a long time to do. When I reached 13 years of age. that became my Saturday morning job for years.

The Well in F19, Potterhanworth Fen

Ben West had a small greenhouse and garden. His main crop was growing tobacco. He would thread the leaves on wire and hang them in the barn until they turned brown and dried out, and then he would pack them in a press. After a month or so they would be in a solid block. Ben would take it out, and slice the block up with a sharp knife. He either rolled the tobacco into fags or smoked it in his pipe. No one else would ever smoke it: you could smell the tobacco a mile away.

There was still no electricity for lights. Mum had to use oil lamps for lighting, and an open fire and cooking range for all the cooking. (After we had been living at Foxes for a few years, we had the house fitted with calor gas lighting.)

There was still no water laid on but

We had a telephone but it was a private one fitted by the estate for the foreman to use to contact the main farm office, or the workshops. We called it the jungle telegraph. It was one of those phones that fitted on the wall and had the mouth-shaped funnel fastened to it. When we used it, we had to wind a handle to make it ring.

With moving to Foxes, which is in Potterhanworth Fen, we children had to change schools so we were sent to Bardney Wesleyan. To get to school we had to walk across the grass paddock to the north of the house then over a plank, crossing the dyke, onto Harold Smithson's farm. For the privilege of using the footpath across his field Dad had to pay their foreman, a Mr Sharpe, 6d for each member of the family per year. Anyone else using it had to pay 6d each time, if they were caught. It wasn't so bad for us as we used it daily because our our milk was left at the end of it, on the side of Bardney Causeway. We could also use it to catch Hudson's or the Roadcar services to Lincoln or Horncastle. There would be a bus every hour at that time. Us kids had a bus pass on Hudson's buses to travel to and from school. Our stop on Bardney Causeway was known as Willoughby's Plank.

We went to Bardney school until secondary modern schools were opened, and Cagthorpe at Horncastle was the Lindsey school that took 11 year olds and over from Bardney. As we lived in Kesteven the transport could not be arranged to take us to Horncastle, so we had to revert back to Nocton School. Kesteven hadn't changed to the secondary modern system at this time so I carried on at Nocton until 1951 when the North Hykeham H.O.R.S.A. (Huts Occasioned by the Raising of School leaving Age) school was opened. This was to take the pupils from the North Kesteven Schools from 14 to15, which was the last year at school for most of us.

During our first few months at Foxes, a new member of staff was hired and he was to become our third lodger and change our lives forever.

Our New Friend Joe

Joe Chamberlain

Joe Chamberlain was hired as second chap to Charlie Cox. This gave us four more heavy horses at Foxes.

Old Joe was to become a great friend of us kids. He was a chap who liked a drop of beer. He invested most of his money in The Chequers at Potterhanworth and The Plough Inn at Potterhanworth Booths. He was a lonely chap so he made his friends behind a glass of beer. All Hudson's bus drivers and conductors knew him well. When he crawled on the last bus at The Plough they all knew he wanted to be off at Willoughby's Plank, often seeing him over the first plank and then he was on his own. It could be the early hours of the morning before he got scrambled across the fields home. My dad would have locked the door by midnight, so Joe would either be in the chaff bin in the stable in the morning or he would be in the barn with Irishmen.

One of his main problems was not having enough money to last the week. He would often borrow off the other workers, but he always paid them back the next Friday, which would be pay day. One of the things he used to do was to jump on the bus for Lincoln, and go to Currys to put a deposit on a new bike. He would pay the instalments for a few months and then get tired of paying so he would ask around the farm to see if any one wanted to buy a bike. He would only ask for enough money to pay the remaining instalments on the bike. I remember at least four men who got themselves a good bike. I got one too, but under different circumstances. One Saturday night after filling himself with beer, he was riding his bike home and coming down the footpath he suddenly had to act to the call of nature. He laid his bike down and wandered a few yards out into the paddock to do his business. On returning to the path he couldn't find his bike so decided to leave it until morning. When he went to collect it in the morning, the horses, that were grazing in the field at that time of year, had walked all over the bike but the only damage was that the wheels were bent. Joe just hung it on the fence and left it. When he came back, Joe came to me in the garden and told me about the bike. He also said, "if you want it boy you can have it." This was one bike he had managed to pay off. I went to look at the bike and decided that it would probably be worth two new wheels. After saving up for a few weeks, I bought two new wheels from George Henson at Bardney and I had myself a nice bike.

Another time coming home with a skin full of beer, the bus dropped Joe off at Battles road end instead of Willoughby's Plank so he found himself down at Battles Farm instead of home. Caught short again he jumped over the fence into Battles pig crew. He'd just got his trousers down when the boar pig, that was in the crew, decided he didn't like old Joe in among his sows, so he decided to do something about it. Heading straight for Joe, he soon had him by the rear and how quick Joe got out of the crew we shall never know. When Joe eventually got home he he was in a poor state, my mum got him dressed up but he had to have two weeks off work.

One way at keeping him off the booze was to volunteer to go out in the stable with him and the cross-cut saw to saw logs. He used to say you always get two warms out of the logs, one when you are sawing them and one when they're on the fire.

Another thing we used to have a bit of fun over was the kitchen, which was long and narrow at Foxes. The open fire and cooking range took about three quarters of the width of it up. There was just room one side for my dad's chair and about a couple of feet the other side (just enough room for an empty orange box). This was the warmest seat in the house in the winter, and it used to be a race for this each night, from the

tea table. Joe used to like to get it, if he could, because it was very convenient for him to spit up the fire back, as another of his likes was chewing tobacco. One of his tricks was: if one of us kids happened to get the box before him, he would dip into his trouser pocket and come out with 1/3d, enough for 10 woodbines. My mum had a tobacco licence to sell fags to the farm men and the fag drawer was in the next room. Joe, of course, would ask the person sitting on the box to get him a packet of fags and, when they got up to get them, he got himself a warm seat until bedtime.

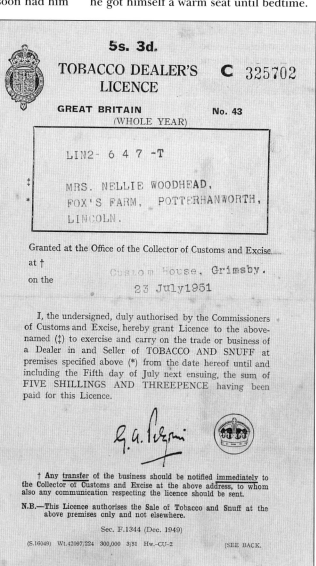

Joe hadn't been on the farm long before he realised the competition between the waggoners and their horses, but he found a simpler way to get extra rations for his horses. He somehow got himself a key to old Ben West's barn, where he used to mix the food for the 100 beasts. Ben would mix up in the afternoon and put the feed in bags ready for carrying out, first thing in the morning, into the tumbrels. When Ben had got off on his bike to Bardney, which he did every night, Joe would be off with his key into Ben's barn. He would take a ladleful out of each bag and take it back to his horses. He did this for years. If Ben had found out he would have murdered Joe because they were never very good friends.

Willow Farm, Dunston Fen, 1940s

Herbert Hodson drives the Caterpillar D7, 1946

Refilling the fuel train, 1950s

Refilling the loco fuel train at Nocton

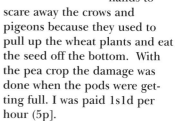

The fuel train leaves Railhead for its trip around the estate

The Changes to Come

I got involved in working on the farm as soon as I was 13 years old. I used to help Ben the garthman to feed the beasts every Saturday and Sunday during the winter season when the beasts were in the crewyard. In the summer time there was always plenty of other work to be done on the farm. I worked all my school holidays and, as soon as I reached 13, along with other school friends, we could get a blue card or permit to allow us to take three weeks off school to help pick the potato crop, during September.

Jack Franklin and potato spinner

Other jobs were crow scaring. We used to have to bike between fields of peas and wheat and shout and clap our hands to scare away the crows and pigeons because they used to pull up the wheat plants and eat the seed off the bottom. With the pea crop the damage was done when the pods were getting full. I was paid 1s1d per hour (5p).

Transferring potatoes from light railway to British Rail at Nocton/Dunston station, 1950s

Another regular job during the corn harvest was following the binder on its first trip around the field and, as the binder threw out each sheaf of corn, I had to grab it to stop it rolling down into the ditch. If any did roll into the ditch, I had to go around the field later with a rake or hand fork and pull the sheaves back on to the field again. Sometimes, if there was water in the ditch, the wheat sheaves were very heavy.

Deering Binder

Loading potatoes for Smith's Potato Crisps en route to the factory

ABOVE: A farm visit at Nocton, 1950s

LEFT: Shanks potato riddle at Nocton, 1950s

Another job was leading the horses when hoeing beet. The horse hoes used to take two and a half rows at each pass across the field. It was important that the horse didn't tread on the row of beet, as each plant was important to make the crop profitable. They used to want at least 75 plants to each chain (22 yards or 20 metres). The man behind, steering the hoe, used to be on piecework rates, so much per acre, so it was important to have the horse ready in the shafts of the hoe when he arrived at work each morning. Us boys were paid 2s 6d per day extra to get the horse tackled up each morning and ready in the field for when the men came to work. We also had to deliver it back to its stable and take its harness off after the day's work.

At this time, the early 50s, there were about 500 head of bullocks on the estate. They would be out to grass, about 50 in a field, and would need moving twice per week to another field of grass. So that was a job for the garthman and a couple of boys. It could be a tiring job. The bullocks would soon run into a beet field or even a corn field and, if the crop was wet with dew or rain, you soon got wet through.

Another harvest job for a boy would be riding on a baler sledge behind a tractor and pick-up baler, collecting the bales as they came out the back of the baler. We used to stack them on the sledge in eights and then release them in a row across the field. With the soil being so high in organic content and poorly drained in the fens

One of seven large potato chitting houses at Nocton, 1950s

at that time, there were ideal conditions for twitch or couch to grow. Since sprays were not being produced at this time, the twitch had to be dragged out on to the top of the ground, it was then chain harrowed by a horse and waggoner plus a boy, who had to walk behind the harrows and when they were full of twitch, the two had to lift up the harrows and release the twitch in rows across the field. It would then be forked up and loaded onto horses and carts and taken to a suitable place for burning. These places were not very easy to find: because of high organic content, the soil would burn as easily as the twitch so could soon develop a deep ground fire.

In July 1952, I was 15 years old. It was time to leave school. There were plenty of jobs to be had at this time, but most would have meant travelling to Lincoln, so I decided to ask for a job on the estate.

The light railway was still being used in a big way but limestone from the Dunston quarry was being hauled by the lorry load to stone the farm roads. Tractors, which were gradually being introduced on the farms, could replace the railway and horses. Up to 1952 there were a few tractors on the estate, a Caterpillar or two, a few Fords and three Allis Chalmers, all on iron wheels. As we stoned the farm roads, rubber tyres had to be thought about. In 1952 the first grey Fergusons with rubber tyres were bought, each with its own three-ton trailer. For each one of these, four horses would leave the farm. This process was to carry on right through the 1950s until we had about 20 Fergusons and trailers. During

Grey Ferguson, HTL 682, 1955

Harvest break for tea: Left to right: M. Reek, R. Sellars, D. Sellars, J. Gray, J. Hardy, J. Reading, A. Franklin, W. Tomlinson, L. Saunby, B. Blackband, K. Wilkinson, L. Woodhead, J. Overton, H. Appleby

this period, with the Ferguson hydraulic system, other implements had been brought in, such as ploughs, drags, mounted harrows and row crop implements.

Also during the 50s, Fordson Major tractors were bought to do some of the heavier work. The Fergusons do the haulage, such as hauling the potatoes and sugar beet off the fields.

By the early 50s the sail reapers were scrapped, their last job on the estate was reaping mustard. The mustard was cut a little under ripe and left about a week to dry out and ripen then it was picked up by combine harvester and the seed bagged on the combine.

The author drives his new Track Marshall 55 with Ransome's two furrow plough, 1961

There were three combines on the estate at that time: two ten ft cut Internationals and one, eight ft cut Massey Harris. Apart from the mustard crop they were used only for the heathland cereals, as the fenland crops were too heavy with straw and were mostly laid flat (there were no growth regulators or straw strengtheners then.)

With the disappearance of the horses, all implements had to be either fitted with drawbars or replaced with mounted implements. As the farm roads were stoned, more lorries were able to deliver directly onto the farm or field. This saved time and labour in not having to transfer from road to rail, and from rail again to tractor trailer, to be taken out to the fields.

The manure could be loaded with a mechanical loader out of the crewyards, instead of by hand.

Tractors were fitted with a drive pulley so they could then replace the steam engines to drive the threshing machine.

The large Caterpillar tractors were brought in, so replacing the traction engines, to do the heavy field cultivations. During the late 50s and early 60s the combine harvesters were replacing the binders.

Riddling potatoes at Nocton, 1940s

Combine drivers: A.Franklin, L. Saunby, W. Franklin, L.Woodhead, L. Massam. Lorry drivers: B. Mitchell, R. Blackband, L. Jacksson

Four Massey 780 specials from the fleet of 13 at Nocton, 1950s

One of three Albion lorries at Nocton, 1950s

Grey Ferguson, 1954, with Massey Harris Binder (the author's first tractor). 1953 Ferguson with Deering Binder in the background.

During the 1960s, sprayers were being introduced. 24 metre Everard Sprayer, Nocton Fen

Thomas potato harvester. Nocton Heath

Mather & Platt super peaviners at work in PF10, Clarks Farm, Potterhanworth Fen, 1978

Beet harvesters were also taking over the hand lifting. The first potato planters and harvesters were being used on the farm, and the pea crop was also being mechanised. Instead of hauling the peas on the vine to a site where there were static viners, mobile viners, pulled by tractors, were coming onto the farm. The peas were still cut and rowed in the field and picked up by the viner.

During this period, a lot of under drainage was being done in the fen and fields were being made bigger, ditches were being filled in. Those that remained were being made larger and easier to maintain, this enabled the four-wheel drive tractors to gradually replace the Caterpillars.

Widening the Smart Drain, Nocton Fen, 1987

New Holland 18ft cut combines, Nocton, 1960s

Irrigation was being used in a big way on the potato crop, beet crop, and also the peas. As we moved into the 1970s a new large drain was cut through the middle of the fen. It was named the SMART Drain, after the managing director Jim Smart. On the Witham end of this drain an electrically driven automatic pump was built to replace the diesel pump on the delf bank.

With the land being drained better, larger machines could be used such as mobile self-propelled pea podders, also larger combine harvesters with 18 ft headers, lorries and larger trailers could travel on the fields.

The Light Railway

Almost all the farms were linked by the railway network and most of the fields also. The system consisted of about six locos, each equipped with small trucks, holding about half a ton: ideal for holding enough rations for a crewyard of beasts and four horses. These rations were delivered round the fen farms each Tuesday. Thursday was fuel day. The fuel train consisted of three trucks, two with large tanks on, one for diesel and one for paraffin, the third truck carried the oils and petrol. Each tractor had its own fuel bowser,

The Iron Bridge that spans the River Witham that was built to carry sugar beet over the river from Nocton Estate in the days of the light railway

which had to be pulled close to the railway line each Thursday morning ready for the fuel train.

Monday was the day when water was delivered to each farm and every house. There was a standpipe at Wasps Nest where the tanks could be refilled and taken around the fen. Each house had a tank for drinking water and a tank for washing water and other uses. These were sited permanently near to the line, most of the water for stock was hand pumped out of ditches or wells. In the summer-time, if the ditches dried up when the stock was out in the fields, then the water train had to be used to take them water also.

The railway was equipped with three-ton open trucks. These were used for car-rying bags of potatoes. Almost all the potatoes were lifted and clamped or graved, as we used to call it, along the side of the railway line, and were riddled or sorted later. About four empty trucks would be left with each riddling gang daily. When they were full, the trucks would be collected and taken to the rail-head at Dunston. There were three men in each riddling gang: one on the scoop forking potatoes onto the riddle; one man on the riddle shaking them and then dropping them into the boy or hopper, which was mounted on the weighing machine. As the potatoes filled the bag on the weighing machine and reached the weight of one cwt (50 KGs], the third man would change the bag for an empty one, tie up the full one and, after being helped by one of the others to get it on his back, he would carry it up a plank, sometimes

over a drain, into the truck.

Some box waggons were used. They carried three ton and were mostly used for corn hauling from the threshing machines.

The open three-ton trucks were also used for hauling sugar beet. A siding could be laid out across the end of the beet field. The beet would be loaded from across the field, brought to the trucks by horse and cart or, later, by the grey Ferguson and transferred. The train would then collect them up to six at a time, (18 ton] and take them to the weigh-bridge which was down near the beet fac-tory. After weighing the beet, it was then forked off the trucks into a pit at the side of the river, where a steel bridge had been built over the river to carry a grab (it is still there at the time of writing]. The grab collected the beet out of the pit, carried it over the river and dropped it into large railway trucks. The beet was then shunted around to the other side of the factory where the men emptied the trucks by hand, placing the beet into the factory flumes.

Another thing the railway had was a carriage, it was called the Queen Mary. This was to carry the bosses and their friends on a pheasant or partridge shoot.

There are still a few signs of the rail-way days left on the farm: part of the met-als crossing a bridge at the bottom of Nocton Fen; one or two water tanks used for collecting rain water around the main workshop buildings at Nocton and Dunston station.

As lorries and tractors were replacing the railway in the late 50s and early 60s, as well as roads having to be laid, water had to be laid to all farmhouses that were still occupied and farmyards that still had beasts or pigs.

As there was no electricity down the fens and no plans to modernise the houses, then as Farmhouses became empty, with the workers moving up into bet-ter houses in the villages, the houses were gradually pulled down.

Riddling potatoes, Dunston Fen

Newark Road Crisp Factory

The last occupants of the Fen farmhouses.

Foxes Farm	W. Woodhead
Bottom Glebe	J. Kingswood
Clarks Farm	Ablewhite
F20 Cottages	Richardson
F20 Cottages	Toynes
Middle Glebe	Claude Smith
Hare Farm	Mrs Rollings
Lark Farm	G. Hubbard
Wharfe Farm	T. Overton
Wharfe Cottage	G. Cooke
Bridge Farm	F. Hewitt
Todds Farm	F. Hewitt
Todds Farm	J. Franklin
Washway Farm	W. Page
Milldrain Farm	F. Tomlinson
Milldrain Cottages	A. Sewell
Milldrain Cottages	Holland
Decoy Farm	F. Tomlinson
Partridge Farm	J. Woodcock
Partridge Bungalow	Ashley
Middle Farm	J. Woodcock
Top Glebe	M. Robert
Nocton Fen Road End	Dickinson
PF3 Cottages	W. Tomlinson
(before they were sold)	
	J. Woodcock
Wasps Nest Cottages	J. Hudson
	Mrs. Rollings
Wasps Nest Four Row	A. Franklin
	J. Woodcock
	Mrs Fields
	Mrs Rollings

During the time the estate was owned by Smith's Potato Crisps, we used to be able to buy a company monthly magazine, this was made up of social news of all the activities and outings throughout all the crisp factories and of course the estate. Anyone could contribute news and so on.

The last horse to be used on the estate in the 1950s

A similar competition to that of the early waggoners existed between the tractor drivers at this time: one or two would write letters or poems to be printed in the magazine. One driver was Wilf Hubbard who was driver of an Allis Chalmers tractor. He wrote the following verse.

An Ode to a Real Tractor

On cold and frosty mornings you'll hear everyone cry.
"Swing up" you Ford Major farmers,
What have the Hubbard Bros. got that others have not,
I'll tell you boys Allis Chalmers.

When harvest comes round and corns lay on the ground,
There are some awful big crops that want clearing,
Who rattles along with a smile and a song?
Why Allis Chal and the Deering.

In the spud business too old "All" sees you through,
At Hilling up she is a winner,
Attached to a drag she never will lag,
And she's second to none on a spinner.

Now I have been told she's nine years old,
They think she is done, that I'll wager,
But I'm willing to bet, that at any job yet,
She would lick the hide off a Ford Major,

When her days really through I know I'll feel blue,
I'll wish I could give her a palace,
For who's the pride of my life next the kids and the wife,
That's right you've guessed it old Allis.

Another expert writer was Bill Redshaw, who wrote the following.

Dear Sir, I write with trembling hand,
To introduce you to our band,
Of real hard workers strong in arm,
Who work for Smiths on Heathlands Farm.

And first, of course, comes Foreman Fred,
Who's always early out of bed
To give us orders, check our sheet,
And fill the lorries up with beet!

And then the ganger Good old Jack,
At any job he'll have a crack,
At stacking, thatching, he is swell,
And picks potatoes just as well.

And next there comes another Fred,
Worrell's his name, and out of bed,
He jumps each morn at just on five,
He really keeps the gang alive!

And then there's Johnny, what a guy,
He's not much more than five feet high,
But he keeps up with Jack and Fred,
Although his face gets rather red.
Next on the list there comes old Perce,
A cockney, but he knows the verse,
On how to feed the cows and bull,
And anywhere he'll give a pull.

Young Ernie is the horseman small,
He feeds the horses in the stall,
And takes them out to work so clean,

No finer horses can be seen.
I must not miss my old pal Harry,
Who's getting on and does not carry,
Such heavy loads as John and Jack,
He's had his share upon his back!

Tom is the shepherd, sheep he feeds,
And looks after their daily needs,
It is a job that calls for skill,
Especially when a sheep is ill.

And on the Fordson Major, Jack,
Lifts up the beet and drops them back,
In drooping rows for men to knock—
His tractor goes just like a clock.

Wilf from the paratroops is back,
He works with Dick, John, Fred and Jack,
And tells them of his mighty deeds,
When they are hoeing up the weeds.

Now Wagg and Dick newcomers are—
But both will say this is by far,
The best farm on the S. P. E.,
And with that sir, we all agree.

And last of all there comes the writer,
He rides all day, the lucky blighter,
Upon his steed the "twenty two",
A Catterpillar, sir, to you,

He harrows, ploughs and drills the land,
And when we're threshing, lends a hand,
To shift the drum from stack to stack,
Then to the railhead takes it back.

And that is our entire happy band
Who work for Smiths on this heathland.

We eat Smith's Crisps in moderation,
Which surely HELP TO FEED THE NATION.

Nocton Fen WI

Another of Bill's is this one:

About the Women's Institute
I put my pen to verse,
The women all belong to it,
Even the district nurse.

The Women's independence
I've heard some fellows say,
Reverse it idle women
But not their tongues that day.

Now take the group of singers
Who practise in the Hall.
They sound like cats at Nocton
Upon the garden wall.

Some say they sing like blackbirds,
But really that's absurd,
They sound just like the Barn Owls,
They do, upon my word.

And on those fateful Thursdays
For tea we look in vain,
They are taking out their curlers
If sunshine, snow or rain.

That night the husband's nursemaid;
He has no time to kill.
He washes up the pots and pans,
In fact, he's never still.

The tiny tots he puts to bed,
And tucks them safely in.
And tells them lots of fairy tales
About old "Gunga Din".

The drama group they take the cake,
They act, or so they say.
They think they're just like Dot Lamour
Except, of course, her pay.

Not satisfied with Thursdays,
They have a gala night.
To go in fancy dresses,
And nearly stay all night.

They have a night for handicrafts,
Its then they learn to sew.
To make hand bags and things like that,
But I believe they go

To have a chat, for it is said
Their needles just won't knit
Until they've had a good chin wag
And found just where to sit.

A stitch in time saves nine they say,
With which I quite agree.
But they don't study time at all;
It's that that puzzles me.

The story it is not complete
Without that cup of tea
'Tis then they says old so and so
Is ageing can't you see?

" It's two years since she bought it."
" It's seen a lot of rain."
" Where did she get those stockings?"
" Those shoes must give her pain."

But after all they're women
We could not do without;
And we are mighty proud of them,
Of that there is no doubt

So let them have their Thursdays,
Their drama and their song,
And all their little parties,
To stop them would be wrong.

Their mottoes, home and country.
Their song Jerusalem.
And now to end this story
I'll say just, God Bless them.

This is another one of Bill Redshaws.

The tractor driver's lament

Oh, Mister Foreman, she's conked out,
The sparking plugs won't spark,
And when the fan is turning,
It whistles like a lark.

The fuel pipes are all clogged up,
At least, that's what I think,
The radiator leaks as well,
It runs just like a sink.
The tappets they're not tapping,
Not regular you know,
I think they're worn completely out,
But maybe that you'll know.

The front wheels they both wobble,
The back wheels they do too.
The air cleaner is broken,
In fact it's right in two.

The gaskets letting oil out,
It really is a game,
It's dropping on the exhaust,
And going up in flame,

The steering wheel is broken,
The clutch sticks sometimes too,
And when she should be stood quite still,
She goes a yard or two.

My seat has come unfastened,
I stand up all day long,
A nut is all that's wanted,
To put to right this wrong.

The wheels they skid like fury,
They make an awful row,
I'd like a Fordson Major
Then I would show them how,

My grease gun is a small one,
A larger one I have seen,
So will you try and buy one,
To put on my machine.

Some new plugs I am wanting,
But railheads far away
And if I go and buy some,
For them myself I'll pay.

She's using oil like blazes,
Three gallons in a day,
And smokes like a steam engine,
Well so my pals all say.

She's like a broken record,
She moves with screech and groan,
In fact, she has been christened
"Old ned the gramophone"

So please send the mechanic
With his magic tin box
He'll cure all her troubles,
And stop those little knocks,

Tell him to bring his little file,
The points want touching up,
One has a little spike on,

The Flood Plain

From Lincoln Boston,
the Witham flows,
besides it's banks,
the wheat field grows.

Past Nocton Blankney
and Walcot Fen,
never to flood this plain again
where once a vast reed bed did stand
the view is now of a different land.

Water sprinklers in the fields
making for even greater yields,
peas potatoes the water grows,
to feed more people - who knows.

Where once the Withams water spread,
it's fenland birds are gone and dead,
pesticides and herbicides,
killed all the insects
and more besides.

The farmers didn't know or care
that they had lost the birds once there,
but change has come we hope to stay,
about time too I hear you say.

Warblers and plovers and harriers too
there back again wheree once they flew,
on Nocton fen in '94 a pair of harriers breed
once more
in May a male was spotted there,
gently floating thrugh the air.

The female sat upon a nest,
while he flew out and did the rest,
each day he flew his mate to feed,
across this fennow not of reed.

In June she sat upon three eggs,
for food from him she calls and begs,
July arrives the hottest yet,
better hot than being wet,
the heat is bad the flys are too,
but soon three chicks come into view.

It's easier now for us to see
for he flys more to feed these three,
in view of our cathedral spires,
he flys all day and never tires,
a man appears with marker peg.

The combine driver up on high must know the
spot unless they fly,
August comes and harvest near,
The birds have flown we need not fear.

All five are flying what a sight
and soon there floating out of sight,
we hope in 1995 that they are back a'gen,
once more to nest in Nocton Fen.

By Dave Satterthwaite who was a friend and bird
watcher who spent a lot of time down Nocton
Fen

Nocton

Ho for the Nocton that once I knew
where on every street corner a majestic tree
grew,
The major oaks, ash, elm and yew,
no more to be seen by me or you.

When the smithy stood on the village street,
and the small holders donkey cart you'd often
meet,
or ploughman return with his leg weary team,
all sights that have gone from our present day
scene.

Our little beck trundled and burbled at speed,
through water cress, kingcups, flag and reed,
where the kingfisher flashed, with his eye like a
bead,
sights that have gone, for we've no time to heed,

To walk throigh the woods in the morning dew,
when the rides were ablaze with Rhododendrons
hue,
and later the scent where the sweet lilies grew,
but alas the chain saw as left but a few.

Or take a stroll where the bluebells display, and
listen awhile to the calls of the jay
or glimpse the red squirrel, as the fur trees sway,
all beautiful sights that are losing the day,

The fat pig was killed and the fries were sent
round,
then sausages, aslet and pork pies abound,
the jams were homemade, for a few pence a
pound,
mouth watering tastes no more to be found.

I know it's no use harking all the way back,
for the time will soon come when I'll have to
pack,
but my Nocton remembered will never retract,
as those pleasant scenes my memory re-enacts.

George started work as a lad at Decoy Farm, Nocoton Fen and was a lodger in the farm house. He told me he used to get up at 5.30 am and had to go out into the grass paddock where the hoses were and get washed in the horse trough, even in the depth of winter with ice on the water, he would go into the farmhouse for breakfast, and the lady of the house would give him a large bowl of hot milk, she would also cut a large thick slice of pure fat bacon and drop it in the bowl of milk, she said, "that will put hairs on your chest milad". George said that when he had eaten that for breakfast he could jump over all the dykes in Nocton fen.

George spent most of his life on the Nocton Estate, from driving the steam cultivators, to Caterpillars and later the large four wheel drive tractors. Sadly he passed away on 7th November 1993 aged 85.

George Wakefield

The others like a cup.

As the old crisp lorries where scrapped, a lot of them where brought on to the estate some where made into 4 wheel trailers for carting produce on the estate, others where used for shelter for the gangs in the potato fields, one is still in use today made into a game cart and to carry bush beaters on shoot days. Can you remember the slogans on the side and rear of the old smiths crisp lorries.

"We Help To Feed The Nation", and on the rear," Please Sound Your Horn We

Old crisp wagons used for shelter in potato field

Wish To Extend To You The Courtesy Of The Road".

My Time on the Estate

For the first two years I was more or less an errand boy, helping the garthman, or the waggoner to tidy up around fields and dykes, helping to lay the limestone on the farm roads, and many other jobs.

When I was 17, in 1954, I was old enough for a driving licence. I was then allocated a new grey Ferguson and after a few months I applied for a driving test. The driving examiner came to Foxes Farm and marked out a road network around the stackyard and in between the stacks. He gave me instructions of where to drive and, after about 20 minutes or so of driving around, he then asked me a dozen or

Ferguson Tractor

so of questions from the Highway Code and I was then a competent tractor driver.

Almost all work on the estate was done at piecework. My jobs, that I did with the Ferguson, were light harrowing, as the corn used to be harrowed in after it was drilled. I was paid 1/- per acre (5p] for this. I also did drilling corn which was a two man job. Someone had to ride on the back of the drill to check that the corn was running down the coulters properly and change the wheel markers over at each end of the field. For this we were paid

AGRICULTURE PIECEWORK RATES-1961

N.F.U. County Branch Areas of Lindsey, Kesteven and Rutland

The representatives of the National Farmers' Union and the National Union of Agricultural Workers for Lindsey, Kesteven and Rutland have agreed on the rates set out in the schedule hereto.

In accordance with the agreement reached, a panel has been set up, composed of representatives of the National Farmers' Union and the National Union of Agricultural Workers. Two members from this panel will be available at any time to help settle on the spot any dispute in the terms of the price schedule. Members are, therefore, advised in the event of a dispute, to contact the N.F.U. County Secretary or the N.U.A.W. District Organiser as the case maybe.

All farmers and workers are urged loyally to adhere to the rates which have been agreed upon between the two Unions.

Signed on behalf of the members of the N.F.U.

H. H. BROWNLOW (*Chairman of Joint Piece Work Rates Committee*)
S. R. SALISBURY (*County Secretary, Rutland County and Stamford Branch N.F.U.*)
N. LOYNES (*County Secretary, Lincolnshire N.F.U.*)

Signed on behalf of the National Union of Agricultural Workers :—

S. BRUMBY (*North Lindsey*)
S. KING (*Kesteven*)
T. BEHARRELL (*Rutland*)
G. CURTIS (*South Lindsey*)

SCHEDULE

LINDSEY

FIRST GRADE LAND—the Warp Land in the Trent Valley and the Isle of Axholme, the Silt Lands South East of Grimsby, the Silt Skirt and Fen Lands in the South of Lindsey.

SECOND GRADE LAND—the remainder of the County of Lindsey.

KESTEVEN

FIRST GRADE LANDS—Rates to apply to the whole of the Fen Lands in the following Parishes : Potterhanworth, Metheringham, Thorpe Tilney, Dorrington, North Kyme, Ewerby, Heckington, Helpringham, Billingborough, Aslackby, Dunsby, Bourne and Dyke, Nocton, Blankney and Linwood, Walcot, Billinghay, Ruskington, South Kyme, Great Hale, Swaton, Sempringham, Dowsby, Hacconby, Thurlby (Bourne), Dunston, Martin and Timberland, Digby, Dogdyke, Anwick, Howell, Little Hale, Horbling, Pointon, Rippingale, Morton, Baston, Langtoft.

SECOND GRADE LAND—Rates to apply to all other lands within the said Division of Kesteven.

RUTLAND

All Lands are classified as SECOND GRADE LAND.

FIRST GRADE LANDS

1. SUGAR BEET. For acreages drilled with 20-inch coulters.

Chopping out (Gapping)	78/- per acre	4/- per acre up or down
Singling	75/- per acre	4/- per acre up or down
Last hoeing and cleaning	71/- per acre	4/- per acre up or down
For completing the job in three operations	224/- per acre	12/- per acre up or down

11/6d. per inch per acre for variation of width of rows, applicable to whole of operation.

Notes : (*a*) We advise our members that the cleaning operations must be completed within a reasonable time.
(*b*) Same rates for 2nd Grade land.
(*c*) Where the employer agrees with a worker for all three operations to be undertaken, the singling operation shall include the removal of weeds from against the plant, and at the instance of the employer, the third operation is later dispensed with, the full rate as for the three operations shall be paid.
(*d*) These prices only apply when beet is chopped out by hand. A price for singling after mechanical gapping to be agreed upon between employer and employee.
(*e*) Where a precision drill is used, the Committee recommends that the DOWN price of 4/- per acre less, be mutually agreed in respect of chopping out and singling.

2. SEEDS

Mustard Seed cutting and tying (Brown)	141/1 per acre	5/- per acre up or down
Mustard Seed cutting and tying (White)	164/6 per acre	10/- per acre up or down
Turnip and Swede Seed cutting and tying	158/2 per acre	5/- per acre up or down
Beet and Mangold Seed cutting, tying and stooking	198/- per acre	5/- per acre up or down
Seed Carting (excluding Clovers)	12/4 per acre per man	6d. per acre up or down per man
Mustard Seed, Turnip and Swede Seed, tying after reaper	Half cost of cutting and tying.	

PRICES for LINDSEY left to individual arrangements.

3. PEAS

Placing on Tripods	34/2 per acre	3/6 per acre up or down
Carting with Elevator (7 forks)	9/1 per acre	1/- per acre up or down
Carting without Elevator (7 forks)	11/11 per acre	1/- per acre up or down
Carting (off tripods, where buck-rake is not used) (7 forks)	11/11 per acre	1/- per acre up or down
Leading off tripods with buck-rake and elevator into stacks with 5 forks (the farmer providing a man to clear and bundle the empty tripods and to place the bundled tripods in a stack or on a trailer)	7/2 per acre per man	9d. per acre up or down

Notes : (*a*) Same rates for 2nd grade land.
(*b*) The erection of Tripods is not a part of the Piece Work operation.

4. CORN — WHEAT, OATS, RYE

Mowing round and tying	5/10 per acre	3d. per acre up or down
Stooking after binder	13/4 per acre	1/- per acre up or down
Carting (including one raking per single gang)	9/- per acre per man	1/- per acre up or down per man

5. CORN — BARLEY

Mowing round and tying	5/10 per acre	3d. per acre up or down
Stooking after binder	12/4 per acre	1/- per acre up or down
Carting (including one raking per single gang)	8/5 per acre per man	1/- per acre up or down per man

Notes : (*a*) This includes making steddle, pegging top of stack, provided straw is conveniently available at site of rick at time of full operation.
(*b*) Corn prices are based upon a gang of six men.
(*c*) Additional men will be required when thrashing direct from the field.

6. THATCHING

9d. per square yard (1st or 2nd Grade land).

7. POTATOES

(a) KING EDWARD AND ROYAL KIDNEY VARIETIES

Picking into carts after plough or spinner	240/2 per acre	5/- per acre up or down
Picking into carts after hoover	191/6 per acre	5/- per acre up or down
Graving, Strawing and Spitting	34/4 per acre	9d. per acre up or down

(b) GLADSTONE, MAJESTIC AND OTHER WHITE VARIETIES

Picking into carts after plough or spinner	211/7 per acre	5/- per acre up or down
Picking into carts after hoover	168/5 per acre	5/- per acre up or down
Graving, Strawing and Spitting	35/3 per acre	10d. per acre up or down

Notes : (*a*) No attempt has been made to agree a price for Potatoes dressed over a riddle and sold in bags ; here it is suggested that a price per ton should be agreed upon by the employer and employee.
(*b*) Price includes twice harrowing after spinner or plough ; once harrowing after hoover.

8. SUGAR BEET (ignoring the width of rows)

Beet lifting, knocking off soil, topping and placing into heaps with ground cleared from tops :—

(a) Commencement of lifting until November 12th	209/3 per acre	5/- per acre up or down
(b) From November 13th to end of campaign	281/- per acre	5/- per acre up or down
Beet filling into carts from HEAPS	55/8 per acre	5/- per acre up or down

Beet lifting into ROWS :—

(a) Commencement of lifting until November 12th	200/9 per acre	5/- per acre up or down
(b) From November 14th until end of campaign	272/5 per acre	5/- per acre up or down
Beet filling into carts from ROWS	68/5 per acre	5/- per acre up or down

Notes : (*a*) The price variations per acre for lifting sugar beet are sufficient for Beet drilled on wider drills.
(*b*) Filling into carts after lifting and topping by machine to be agreed between employer and employee.

SECOND GRADE LANDS

9. SEEDS

Mustard Seed cutting and tying (White)	159/8 per acre	10/- per acre up or down
Turnip and Swede Seed cutting and tying	153/8 per acre	5/- per acre up or down
Beet and Mangold Seed cutting, tying and stooking	177/6 per acre	5/- per acre up or down
Seed Carting (excluding Clovers)	10/8 per acre per man	6d. per acre up or down per man
Mustard Seed, Turnip and Swede Seed tying after reapers	Half cost of cutting and tying.	

PRICES for LINDSEY left to individual arrangements.

10. CORN — WHEAT, OATS, RYE

Mowing round and tying	5/3 per acre	3d. per acre up or down
Stooking after binder	10/9 per acre	1/6 per acre up or down
Carting (including one raking per single gang)	8/5 per acre per man	1/6 per acre up or down per man

11. CORN — BARLEY

Mowing round and tying	5/3 per acre	3d. per acre up or down
Stooking after binder	9/6 per acre	1/6 per acre up or down
Carting (including one taking per single gang)	7/7 per acre per man	1/6 per acre up or down per man

Notes : As per Grade 1 Lands (see items 4 and 5).

12. POTATOES

(a) KING EDWARD AND ROYAL KIDNEY VARIETIES

Picking into carts after plough or spinner	216/5 per acre	15/- per acre up or down
Picking into carts after hoover	173/5 per acre	15/- per acre up or down
Graving, Strawing and Spitting	30/11 per acre	2/- per acre up or down

(b) GLADSTONE, MAJESTIC AND OTHER VARIETIES

Picking into carts after plough or spinner	202/7 per acre	15/- per acre up or down
Picking into carts after hoover	164/1 per acre	15/- per acre up or down
Graving, Strawing and Spitting	33/9 per acre	2/6 per acre up or down

Notes : (*a*) No attempt has been made to agree a price for Potatoes dressed over a riddle and sold in bags ; here it is suggested that a price per ton should be agreed upon by the employer and employee.
(*b*) Price includes twice harrowing after spinner or plough ; one harrowing after hoover.

13. SUGAR BEET

Beet lifting, knocking off soil, topping and placing into heaps with ground cleared from tops :—

(a) Commencement of lifting until November 12th	191/- per acre	15/- per acre up or down
(b) From November 13th to end of campaign	258/5 per acre	15/- per acre up or down
Beet filling into carts from HEAPS	53/2 per acre	5/- per acre up or down

Beet lifting into ROWS :—

(a) Commencement of lifting until November 12th	184/5 per acre	15/- per acre up or down
(b) From November 13th to end of campaign	247/7 per acre	15/- per acre up or down
Beet filling into carts from ROWS	63/4 per acre	5/- per acre up or down

Notes : (*a*) and (*b*) as for 8 above.

14. MANGOLDS. For acreages drilled with 20-inch coulter.

Gapping and singling	111/6 per acre	5/- per acre up or down
Hoeing	70/- per acre	5/- per acre up or down
Filling into carts	60/3 per acre	5/- per acre up or down
Lifting, topping into heaps and leafing	143/3 per acre	5/- per acre up or down
Topping into rows	110/1 per acre	5/- per acre up or down

2/6d. per inch variation for width of rows.

15. TURNIPS. 20-inch coulter with 10-inch blade.

Chopping out for sheep — 47/- per acre
1/- per inch variation for width of rows.

16. SWEDES. 20-inch coulter.

Gapping — 57/6 per acre
1/6d. per inch variation for width of rows.
Chopping and Singling — 87/6 per acre
1/6d. per inch variation for width of rows.

0.71

The farm workers union would issue these rates each April.

1/9d per acre (8p].

We would be spreading crewyard manure. The foreman would come to the field and offer us so many £s to spread the heap that had been carted and stacked in the corner of the field earlier in the year. We used a sail reaper to cut mustard. The Ferguson replaced the horses on the Binders at harvest time. We harrowed the wheat and other cereals after they got nicely growing, this was to try to destroy any weeds that were growing (there was very little spraying done at this time). We also harrowed and Cambridge rolled the potato ridges, just before the potato shoots came through the ground.

In the early 50s, with the government encouraging farmers to increase output, one of the grants available was for drainage and the Fens of Lincolnshire and our area were certainly in need of that.

Most of the underground tile draining was put in by hand so this meant thousands of clay land tiles were needed. These were delivered by lorry and all had to be handled individually off the lorries and then carted out to the fields. This

Jack Brumpton, shepherd sets off on his rounds

Potato planting: E. Redshaw on tractor, A. Franklin, D. Woodcock and M. Carr on planter

Cramer potato planter, W. Franklin driving Massey Ferguson tractor.

the field was. There was no way to take levels other than by taking some water across the field and pouring it along the bottom of the channel you were digging. The Ferguson and trailer would be used to cart out the clay tiles which would be stacked in heaps along the side of the channels, for the men to use.

With the fens being poorly drained, the acid subsoils had very low pH. Before crops like sugar beet could be grown the pH had to be raised to 7.5 or 8. The way we did this was by carting waste lime from Bardney Sugar Factory to spread on the fields @50 tons per acre. Quite a lot of this was carted by Ferguson trailer: three tons per load.

was another job for the Ferguson and trailer. The drainage channels were dug by two men in each gang and were mostly between three and four feet deep, depending on te depth of the dyke that the water had to drain to and, of course, how level

Seed potatoes would be carted out of the glasshouses, where they had been stored in heat during the winter to enable them to be nicely chitted. Again by Ferguson trailer, they would be carted in chitting trays and put out along the potato ridges for the men or women to plant.

With the new hydraulic system on the Fergusons there were quite a lot of new implements becoming available: ploughs, drags, beet drills, reapers, beet hoes and weeders to use instead of harrows, and also mechanical potato planters.

In the late 50s, I was allocated a larger tractor. This was a Fordson, twice the horsepower of the Ferguson, 50hp. I could use larger implements such as a four-row potato planter instead two row; a three or four furrow plough instead of two and a larger corn drill. The piece-work rate was £2/8d per acre 13p).

Then in the early 60s two

Deepening the dykes with the Atlas excavator, A. Franklin and P. Chapman

new Track Marshalls were bought for the fens. These were 55hp, this enabled us to

Track Marshall ploughing

get on earlier with most jobs. I could deep plough and subsoil in one pass, and earn 7/6d per acre 37p.

At this time, came one the happiest times of my working life. The farm bought a Ford County Crawler and they advertised for an experienced driver. Onto the estate came a person whom we called 'Hairy Ben'. He was a laugh a minute and if you needed a hand, he was the man. Some of the things he said and did you

Peter Gash, Herbert Hodson, Jack Worrel, Walter Tomlinson, J. Reading, P. Doughty, J. Blackband

would think were stupid but with us all working hard and for long hours, we needed a bit of fun and a laugh.

When we were ploughing, after the sugar beet, for autumn wheat, it would

sometimes be very dry and hard and we would have trouble getting our plough to penetrate the ground, so we would hang two or three four-stone weights on the rear of the plough.

On one occasion Ben and I were ploughing together in the same field. We were having problems getting the ploughs to penetrate when into the field came Nobby George the head foreman.

He came straight up to Ben and said, 'Where's ya fower ston weights?' Ben

George Chambers and Bill Woodhead planning the working day

Four Ford 5000s and two Muir-Hill 101s hoping to be ploughed up by Christmas, 1970s

stared at him and said, "Bugger me George, I took them out my pocket this morning".

On another occasion it was a wet day, not fit for any landwork (what we called a by-day.] On these sort of days most of the workers who were working nearby would make for the glasshouse where it was warm, especially in the winter, as there would be a brazier or two burning. With these glasshouses having just a soil floor and being heated through the winter, there would be about two or three inches of dust on the floor of each glasshouse.

This particular day most of us workers were all in the glasshouse out of the rain. Down the farm road came Hairy Ben on his Francis Barnet motorcycle. We opened the door for him but instead of just riding steady into the glasshouse, he came flying in at speed, down to the far end of the glasshouse and back. Now you can imagine what it was like with all that dust: we all had to stand out in the rain until it settled.

Between the spring work and harvest, most of the men on the farm would be doing manual work such as gapping beet. On one occasion there were about 20 of us sitting down having our lunch break along a large drain side. It was a windy day and the wind blew one man's hat off. It dropped in the water. Ben jumped up and, grabbing his hoe to reach it, said, 'I'll get it.' The hat was floating nicely on the surface of the water but instead of being gentle and picking it up, Ben pushed down with his hoe and pushed it under the water first. The owner said, 'You silly bugger you're a bloody maniac.'

Another time, during the winter period when there wasn't any landwork going on, most of us were riddling potatoes out of clamps sited by the farm roads. Ben and I were helping a regular gang to riddle. In the gang was an elderly chap called Bill, now Bill had got an urgent appointment at 3.30 on this afternoon so he asked my dad, who was farm foreman, if he could go home an hour early. My father had said yes, that would be OK. Now at dinner time Bill had told us about this, and said, 'if Nobby George is about

(the head foreman] keep quiet and I'll try and slive off without him seeing me.' Sure enough Nobby came and was picking off the riddle, old Bill managed to get on his bike and was just riding away when Ben shouted 'goodnight Bill.' Bill turned round and shook his head and said, 'dear, oh dear', and away he went. Nobby reared his head and said, 'where the bloody hell is he going?' When Bill came to work next morning he said, 'if I had had a gun I would have shot him.'

Old Bill used to join Ben and me mowing dyke sides during the late spring. Sometimes Ben would have Bill on the back of the Francis Barnet with a couple of scythes on his back. Off like the clappersthey would go to the far end of the field. We had some happy times together.

Once, when we were riddling potatoes another elderly worker came to help us take the soil off the clamp.The gang were riddling on piecework. Nobby George came and he was picking off as usual. A lorry came for a load of potatoes. Nobby shouted to the old chap Bill to come and help load this lorry. Bill said, 'I aren't doing that, I'm only on day work.' Nobby replied, 'if Mr Ireson hears you, you'll be on your bike!' (Mr Ireson was Farm Manager.]

Myself, Ben and old Walt, one of the garthmen, were moving about 50 bullocks from one grassfield to another. We had to cross a wooden bridge over a big drain. Now it was always difficult to get animals to cross bridges when they could see the water between the planks of wood. Old Walt kept saying, 'quiet, steady, be quiet.' This just suited Ben. Eventually one or two of the leading bullocks looked as though they were going onto the bridge. Here was an opportunity for Ben to have a bit of fun, he shouted, 'Ya ooh!' The bullocks turned round and ran like the clappers. I'll not mention what Walt said. Of course we all had to go back and round them up, which is very difficult after they have been frightened.

With me driving a crawler, I was free to drive a combine harvester during the cereal harvest, at this time we had 13 Massey 780 specials. Harvest days were very long, we would start as soon as it was dry in the morning and work until dark. Later, lights were fitted so we could work until 11pm.

In the early 60s we grew quite a lot of oats. When it came to harvest time they were mostly laid flat to the ground, so we needed really good dry weather. When the oats were really ready and we could see several dry days ahead, the dryers would be changed over and all the combines would be cutting these crops. There was no special knocking off time, we just carried on into the night until the dew came down and stopped us. Most of the oats were grown on the really high organic soils, which made them more difficult to cut. They were more often pulled up rather than cut. If this happened then a

Mr Rod Hargreaves, Farm Manager at Nocton, late 1950s to mid 1990s

larger Bamford Clayes replaced these 13 Massseys. When they arrived, the Bamfords were painted with the Smith's Crisp Diamond on the rear. After these

Left: Bamford Claeys combines

Right: Muir-Hill 101, cultivating

lot of the crop was lost. Coming out of one field, on one particular day, we seemed to have cut it fairly quickly. As we met at the corner of the field to discuss where we were going to next, I said Jim, who was one of the other drivers, 'Gosh we soon cut that field!' Jim said, 'cut it? We've knocked the bugger down!' Later, nine

came 15-foot cut New Holland Claysons. Later came 18-foot, then 20-foot, and finally 24-foot. The early ones didn't have cabs for the drivers. When cabs finally arrived it was a godsend. Each time after when combines were renewed, the cabs got better. Gradually all controls and adjustments were done from the cab. They were

CONTRACT of EMPLOYMENT Act 1963

This statement sets out the particulars of the terms and conditions on which:—

1. We, **SMITH'S POTATO ESTATES Ltd.,**
   THE ESTATE OFFICE,
   NOCTON, LINCOLN

2. are employing you .... **Leonard Woodhead.**

3. as at .... **14th March 1966.**

4. The employment began on ...... **Over 5 years.**

5. **REMUNERATION.** Your rate of pay is in accordance with that set out in the appropriate Agricultural Wages Board Order, a copy of which is available for reference at the Estate Office **plus £2.0.0d.**
Any future change in the Order will be recorded within ONE MONTH of the change in the register kept at the Estate Office and will be similarly available for reference. For work done at "Piece-work" rates, the rates of payment will be in accordance with the schedules prepared and issued by the Joint Piece-work Rates Committee of the Lindsey, Kesteven and Rutland Areas as agreed between the representatives of the National Farmers' Union and the National Union of Agricultural Workers. Copies of these schedules are available for reference at the Estate Office. Other Piece-work rates not included in the schedules of the Lindsey, Kesteven and Rutland Areas to be arranged between Employer and Employee to their mutual satisfaction and to be recorded in the Wages Register.

6. You will be paid WEEKLY and on FRIDAY.

7. **HOURS of WORK.** Your normal hours of work and meal-breaks are as set out in the wages register, available for reference at the Estate Office. Any seasonal variation and any future change in normal hours will be recorded therein within ONE MONTH. Overtime will be worked if required and this will be paid for at the rates set out in the appropriate Agricultural Wages Board Order.

8. **HOLIDAYS.** Your entitlement to holidays and holidays with pay are as set out in the appropriate Agricultural Wages Board Order.

9. **SICKNESS or INJURY.** No wages are payable during absences from work.

10. **PENSION SCHEME.** Your employment is not covered by a pension scheme.

11. **LENGTH of NOTICE.** You are entitled to receive ONE WEEK'S notice of termination, increasing to TWO WEEKS after two years service and FOUR WEEKS after five years service.
You are required to give the Company ONE WEEK'S notice of termination.

12. **SERVICE HOUSES.**
    a You are required, for the better performance of your duties, to live as a service occupier in a house provided by the Company.
    b. The weekly value of such house shall be reckoned at the amount at which it is valued under the appropriate Agricultural Wages Board Order. Such amount shall be payable weekly by you to us and will be deducted from wages.
    c. You are required to keep the house in good clean condition and to cultivate the garden properly and to vacate the house on termination of the Contract of Employment.

Signature of Employer or Agent .... SMITH'S POTATO ESTATES LTD.

Jim Smart

Date 14th March 1966.

MANAGER.

Smiths Crisp's Diamond

During the 70s, under the management of Jim Smart and Mr Rod Hargreaves, the estate, especially the fenland, was improved tremendously. This was mainly due to the under drainage and the spreading of sludge lime, obtained from Bardney Sugar Factory, and the deep subsoiling, which enabled the plant roots to move easily and more widely through the soil.

also fitted with air conditioning.

In the meantime four-wheel drive trac-

Mr W. Tomlinson with Muir Hill 121, four wheel drive

tors were replacing the crawlers. There were some Samme tractors, some John Deers and then the Muir Hill.

This seemed to be the way things were going, as these tractors were more versatile: by using mounted implements and with having rubber tyres, it was easy to move across the whole estate. The Muirhills could do all the jobs the crawlers

did and more besides, such as pulling large potato harvesters and Mather and Platt pea-viners.

During my time driving a Muirhill, I did all those jobs and used a large hydraulic plough. We also started to do more sub soiling. Since the farmers were seeing the advantages of four-wheel drive, almost all manufacturers started to produce them.

In February 1971, the Wasps Nest Foreman (Section A] was off work sick and he retired. I applied for the job and was accepted. This was a time of great improvement on the estate, with

Mather and Platt Pea VIners and Reco Pea Cutters

Digging the reservoir, April 1987

The Witham Extraction Point

The Wasps Nest transfer pumps at the reservoir

irrigation starting to be used, following the advantages of quick drainage, and the need for larger fields.

A large drain was cut down the centre of the fen from the rivers almost to Wasps Nest and on the eastern end, near the river, an automatic pumping station was built. This meant that a lot of the under drainage had to be modernised. It also meant that the smaller dykes had to be made to fall towards the new drain.

In 1973, my dad, who was foreman on Section C, reached the age of 65. In the February he retired. I was asked to take on the acreage that he had been responsible for, which I did. In 1975 the estate was sold. Our new owners were British Field Products, a subsidiary of GRE Insurance. In 1987 a large investment was put into irrigation.

A reservoir was built half way between the fen and heath. Water was to be pumped out of the River Witham into the Smart drain. It then flowed three quarters of the length of the fen as far as the Partridge Farm ,where it was pumped over a dam to lift the levels by about six feet. This allowed the water to reach the Wasp Nest where it entered a small reservoir from which point the water was pumped into a 12 inch main, to take it up to the large reservoir. From the 10 million-gallon reservoir, water was pumped up to a computerised pumping station on the heath and then pumped into a ring main around the heath.

During the period from 1971, when I

One of the 13 hose-reels used on the estate

became Farm Foreman, the area of land I was responsible for increased from around 900 acres 4000. Eventually I moved on to being assistant crops manager to the whole estate.

The estate was sold again in 1995. After two years under the new owner, I was made redundant, giving me 45 years on the estate.

My Time in Nocton Village

In December 1960 I got married and we moved to Main Street, Nocton. In 1963 Nigel was born, and in 1965 our daughter Diane.

At the time the village community was

L. Woodhead and Major Robert Rose USMC

The hospital closed in March 1983

still mostly estate workers, as the estate owned most of the houses.

The RAF Hospital was operating so there were quite a lot of civilians from the village with jobs there. When the children started Nocton school, my wife, Pauline, started a part-time job there.

Village life was great for the kids. They could move safely around the village to play with friends. Pauline and I joined the social club and Pauline joined the WI.

There was a great community spirit. Everybody would do anything for the village or residents and would never look for anything in return. When half-term came round just before Guy Fawkes Day, the children, with the aid of a four-wheel truck, would visit all the houses in the village to collect any burnable rubbish to make a bonfire in Elkingtons Paddock. They seemed to get as much fun out of this as they did out of the bonfire.

In June 1977, the village residents got together to form a committee to organise a celebration for the Queen's Jubilee anniversary day. I organised the village sports, another person organised a village barn dance and hog roast which was held in Elkingtons Barn. The sports day was so successful that I carried it on for several years. As our children grew up and lost interest in the sports, I gave up as organis-

L. Woodhead and the village school headmaster, Mr Twells, distributing the prizes to the winners at the Queens Silver Jubilee Sports Day, Nocton, 1977.

er. Philip Franklin carried it on for a few years.

After giving up the sports, I took on the role as entertainments' organiser for the village social club. During the next few years we had country music shows, discos, hypnotists and all sorts of entertainment. I also had a spell on the Parish Council and with the help of the Nocton Estate Management, David and Gill Rumbelow, the estate shepherd and his wife, Sheep Dog Trials were held at Nocton for over 20 years. Contestants came from all over

Nocton Sheepdog Trials 1975.
Daisy Wakefield, Sally Bellamy, Eileen Moulds, Pauline
Woodhead, Ann Moulds, Freda Redshaw, Mrs. Smart,

the country, and as far away as Wales and Cumbria, to compete. Many prizes and donations were given by local businesses,

P. Woodhead, S. Kissane, D. Woodhead, G. Rumbelow, A.
Brown serving refreshments at Sheepdog Trials 1990

and all profits from the event were given to the Nocton Village Hall.

In 1971, we moved house to live in part of the Manor House, where we stayed for over 25 years.

We then moved to our present home in Metheringham. The Nocton village has changed tremendously over the last few years, the entire farm buildings in the village have been converted into dwellings, and any spare ground has been used as a building plot.

We have to accept change but with the change came the disappearance of the community gatherings. The farm buildings, which were mostly made of stone,

were being converted into houses. They became attractive dwellings but were too expensive for local workers, therefore village life completely changed. Southerners and city dwellers moved in, and in several cases both parents were going out to work. The village life that we used to be part of disappeared forever. The English way of ethnic cleansing? I agree that these old buildings should be converted, but the dwellings could have been made smaller, to keep some of the old village characters in the area.

The Estate crops over my 45 Years

POTATOES

In the early 1950s, when I started work, around 900 acres of potatoes were grown on the estate, all of which were for Smith's Potato Crisps. New seed was bought each year, from Scotland, to be planted on the limestone heath part of the estate, and out of the yield of these was taken enough seed to plant the acreage in the fens. When the heath potatoes were graded or riddled in September or October, they were put into chitting trays and carted down the fens to be stacked up outside the glasshouses until the night frosts came, then they were moved and stacked inside to be protected from the winter. Coke braziers were used on cold nights.

Most of the potato land would have had several tons per acre of farmyard manure spread on it during the autumn, and then it would be ploughed 10 to 12 inches deep. Next, the field was dragged to help it to dry out. The field would then be ridged and a fishmeal-based fertiliser would be applied, ready for the seed potatoes to be planted. The seed would be carted out from the glasshouse by horse and cart and stacked in piles across the field. Gangs of men or women then planted them down the ridges. Two horses pulling a three-row ridger would follow the planting, to split the ridges to cover up the potatoes. I was always amazed with the horses: they had to walk on the top of the ridges so they didn't move the potatoes that had been planted in the bottom of the ridges.

Just before the potatoes emerged, the ridges would be rolled down and then chain harrowed to move any weeds (there were no chemical sprays for the control of weeds at this time). As the potatoes grew, the field would be skerried or cultivated between the rows several times, until just before the potatoes met in the rows, giving full ground cover. They would then be hoed by hand to take out any weeds, after that a three-row ridger would be used to ridge them up.

Gradually a fungicide was introduced to prevent blight; this was always applied in the early hours when the dew was still on the leaves so the powder stuck to them. The dusting machine was pulled by one horse and had booms, similar to the sprayers, about the width of ten 28-inch rows. The potatoes were left until September, when the tops would start to die off. As soon as this happened they

Bob Peak emptying hampers into the trailer

would start spinning them out for the gangs to pick them.

The length of the potato rows would be measured and divided up into retches of six or eight, depending on how many pickers there were in the gang. The man with the spinner would spin out a row across the field. The pickers would then spread out across the field, taking a retch

each, which was marked with a stick. As workers picked the potatoes into baskets, a man with a horse and cart would come down the field and empty the baskets, ready for the next row.

The potatoes were taken to the end of the field where there would be a railway line or a stone road. Here they would either be riddled for daily despatch to the crisp factories, or there would be a man

Percy Ward and Bill Jackson

waiting to make a clamp, which would be about six feet high and pointed at the top.

The potatoes would then be covered with straw and later about 12 inches of

A women's potato picking gang on the Nocton Estate,

soil would be piled on the top of the straw, to keep out the winter frosts.

As the horses were replaced by tractors, mechanisation began: the spinner was changed to a hoover to lift the potatoes gently out of the ridge; the horse and cart was replaced by a tractor and trailer; later the first potato planters came along. These were three-row machines. Three men sat at the rear feeding the potatoes into revolving cups. As the wheel turned, at one point the potato was allowed to drop down into the ridge, the machine had either ridging bodies or discs to split the ridges covering up the potatoes. This was later replaced by unmanned planters. When that time came, chitted potatoes were not required as the machine would knock off the chits. This made the glasshouses obsolete. Insulated seed stores where the potatoes were stored in bulk replaced them and the temperature was controlled automatically with refrigeration and air circulation.

Eventually the planter also applied the fertiliser and made the ridges. Sprays were

Two row potato harvester

introduced to replace the cultivations and hand hoeing.

Next appeared the potato picker or harvester. The first one at Nocton was a two row, manned harvester, a Shotbolt. It was built around a Nuffield tractor and could accommodate six picking off. Then came the Krakia, which was a two row and was adapted to carry two for picking off. Next to these came the Haymac, which were unmanned, and finally the Grimme all-rounder that was a manned harvester. Controlled potato stores were built to store the ware. This cut out the need for clamping in the field, which was a great step forward, as the bulk of the potatoes were graded out during the winter months. When the weather was cold the store was better for any staff needed for this operation.

Irrigation came along in the 60s, boosting yields from around 10 tons per acre to 17 or even 20 at times. With the heavy cropping of potatoes, eelworms or

nematodes began to multiply in the soil and this affected the yield, so a nemeti-

Amac potato harvester, 1980

cide had to be worked into the seedbed when planting.

When the harvesters came along the potato tops had to be burnt off with acid and pulverised to help them through the harvester.

SUGAR BEET

Up until the mid 1950s, sugar beet could not be grown on the high organic fens, as they were too low in pH. This was the time when 1000s of tons of waste lime was brought in to spread on the fields. Eventually the pH levels were brought up to 7.5 or 8, which meant we were able to produce reasonable crops of beet almost anywhere on the estate. Owing to the rise and fall of the water levels, the lime still has to be applied annually, in some parts.

When I started on the estate in 1952, beet was grown quite differently from the way it is today. The land was ploughed 10 to 12 inches deep during November or December, in the hope of getting some good winter frosts to break it down well. In the following March about one ton of basic fertiliser, this was mostly in 18-stone bags (115 kg], per acre was spread on the fields. (At that time the experts used to say you needed to give it plenty of roll.) After the fertiliser was spread the tractor or spreader wheelings would be dragged out, then it would be harrowed in both directions to get it as level as possible. Next a couple of passes with a Cambridge roll, then another two passes with the harrows and finally two more passes with the rolls would be made.

It would then be ready for drilling. With the land being fairly firm, the beet would be set out of the ground. This made it easier to hand pull, after it had been ploughed out. The drills at this time were five rowed, 18 inches apart. One man followed the drill, with a boy leading the horse to help keep straight. The seed was almost as big as a pea seed, but it was

down the row, and a man to walk behind to steer the hoe.

With the beet being so thick in the row it needed spacing out to let the remaining plants grow to a reasonable size, so the next job was gapping. Gangs of men or women did this by using long handled draw hoes, with usually an eight-inch blade. This was done at piecework of 78/- per acre. (£3.90p]. The next pass was to single the clumps that were left down to one plant, each being eight inches apart. The rate was 75/- per acre (£3.75p]. Later the gangs would go through the crop again and hoeing out any weeds that had

12 metre set of Cousin Cambridge rolls

a cluster of maybe eight beet seed in each and was sown continuously along the row.

As the beet emerged, the next operation was to cultivate between the rows to move any weeds that were growing, as there was no sprays at this time. A horse hoe did this operation. The machine was a two and a half row machine pulled by one horse, with a boy to lead the horse

grown in the rows. The rate for this job was 71/- per acre. (£3.55p]. During this period, before the crop reaching full ground covered the horse hoe would go through all the beet crops as many times as possible to remove any weeds.

The sugar beet factory campaign would start about early October and carry on until all beet had been delivered and processed, which would take until late February or early March. The harvesting programme would start with the beet being ploughed out. A gang of men would follow, pull the beet up, knock off the soil and lay the beet in row. They would then turn round, chop off the top and leave the beet in heaps, for a piecework rate of £10.9/- per acre (£10.45p]. Next came a horse and cart, the beet was picked up with a fork and loaded into the cart. The piecework rate was 55/8d (£2.79p) per acre.

The beet was then taken to the nearest railway line, where it was loaded onto the three ton trucks. If the field had a line running past it, a siding was often laid on to the headland so as not to interfere with other passing trains.

As soon as six trucks were loaded, along would come a train to collect them and haul them down towards the factory. Each truck would be weighed on our weighbridge, which was situated just over the Fen road, where the filter beds are now. After weighing, the beet was then taken down to the river where we had a grab to carry the beet over the Witham. The trucks were emptied by hand into a small pit. The grab would come over the bridge, take the beet out of the pit and carry it over to the factory. On the factory side of the river was a siding linked to The London North Eastern Railway. A grab dropped the beet into trucks on this side and British Sugar had a small shunting engine to move the beet round to the flumes. It was at this point that a sample was taken to test for sugar content, which would determine the price for the grower. Here the beet was again emptied by hand

ABOVEand BELOW:One of the first Catchpole beet harvesters at Nocton, 1950s

BSC factory at Bardney, 1936

Standan Solo Beet Harvesters, D. Sellers J. Overton

into the flumes so that it could be washed into the factory.

As we modernised, first a tractor replaced the horse plough; a grey Ferguson and trailer replaced the cart; and beet lifting machines came along. The first we had were single row machines, Catchpole. These machines were pulled by a 28hp Fordson Major but they also needed a man to steer the machine. As well as steer the machine, the driver had to pull a lever to clear the tops in order to discharge the beet in rows across the field, from where it was still collected by hand and put into trailers.

By this time the farm roads were being stoned to make them suitable for lorries. At first the beet was still carried by rail but, owing to the closing of our weigh-bridge, a large lay-by and railway sidings were built in Foxes road end and here the beet was transferred from rail to lorry. It was then taken the short distance by road round to the Factory.

The next machines to come along were Catchpole Cadets, which were similar to the others. They topped and lifted the beet but also cleaned most of the soil. A tractor and trailer ran along side to collect the beet instead of it being discharged on to the ground.

About this time the roads were stoned to most farms and fields so the lorries could replace the trains. The beet could

Moreau six-row beet harvester, 1980. Jim Hardy, Jess Overton

J. Overton loads the lorry, A. Bee is the lorry driver

be loaded straight from the field onto a lorry.

The next step in this part of the beet harvest were that Standen Solo Harvesters. These were fine machines, which replaced the older machines. When the beet cam-paign came round, Ferguson 35s were taken to the workshop where the wheels were taken off and the tractor was mounted on the top of the Solo Harvester to become its power source so making this a one-man machine.

We had six of these machines, which were single row and could lift and clean three acres each per day. They had a holding tank of about one ton. When this was full the harvester was driven to the lorry, that would be waiting nearby, and the machine could elevate the beet straight into the lorry.

In my opinion from this stage to the present day the beet harvest has not improved.

After these machines came the multi-row harvesters. From here on the empha-sis was for tonnage or acreage rather than quality clean beet. The first multi-row we had was a six-row Moreau: it topped, lift-ed and loaded into a trailer running alongside. It covered about 20 acres per day. This beet was mostly dirty, so from here on it had to be dumped and put through a cleaner loader before the facto-ry would accept it. Whereby the Solos needed just six machine drivers plus three lorry drivers to deliver beet to the factory, we now needed: one harvester driver, two tractor drivers, one driver to heap up the beet on specially made concrete pads, another driver to drive a loader to feed the beet into a special cleaner loader plus 2 lorry drivers and on most occasions 2 to 4 picking rubbish or soil off the cleaner. Then there's the problem of disposing of

Herriau six-row topper. L. Massam

the soil, and another tractor and trailer and driver is needed.

Other multi-rows we tried were the Herriau system which comprised of, one tractor pulling a six-row topping machine, another pulling a six-row lifter, lifting the beet and then laying it back on the ground for a third machine to pick it up and load

Herriau loader. E. Sellars, P. Freestone with trailer

G. Tomlinson heaps up the beet with the Volvo loader

Herriau six-row lifter. R. Sellars

into a tractor and trailer, which then took it to a concrete pad.

The second Hall field is cleared of trees and the grass ploughed up, 1960s. Fred Wilkinson with dozer

Moving back to how other stages of the growing of the crop have changed, the biggest changes came in the seed. In the late 1970s rubbed seed was coming on the market. This was the large clump of seed being rubbed together in a machine until most of the seeds were single. This enabled better drills to be brought in, and the seed could be drilled thinly down the row, which gave a better chance of leaving single plants when gapping. Then followed, as it is today, pelleted seed, whereby each single seed was enclosed in clay or gypsum to make nice small balls with the seed in the centre. These were all made exactly the same size, so a drill could be made to space the seed in the soil at whatever distance was required. With this system there was no need for gapping by hand anymore. The cultivations have been reduced to try to get less compaction and so enable the roots to move more freely in the soil, and also to get the beet to grow deeper in the soil for the mechanical toppers to do a better job.

Five-row steerage hoes replaced the horse hoes, with a tractor driver and a man riding on the following hoe to steer so the beet didn't get cut up. These were soon replaced by five-row hoes being fixed under small tractors, such as small John Deers or Allis Chalmers. The hoes could then be steered from the tractor seat, making it a one-man operation. As the tractors got larger, then the beet drills and hoes got wider Today you see mostly 18-row machines.

During the late 70s and into the 80s, weed sprays or pesticides, being produced to control some of the fen weeds, were not very successful for a start, but gradually they have improved. When they were first used on the beet crop they were sprayed with a four inch band of spray down each row, so the beet hoe was still needed. As the chemical improved and the labour thinned out, the beet was sprayed overall. Now the tractor hoes are hardly ever used.

The Pea Crop

When I started work in the early 1950s the few peas that were grown on the estate were under contract for John Morrell's Cannery at Bardney. When these were ready, late June or early July, Morrells would order so many loads per day. These would be cut with a grass reaper, loaded by men with hay forks, onto trailers, and then taken to Morrells at Bardney where they were fed into two static pea-viners on their way into the cannery. The tractor driver had to load up the thrashed vine and brings it back to be disposed of on the farm.

We also grew a few broad beans at this time, but these had to be pulled by hand as they were ordered at so many bags per day.

The next change in the harvest was when Morrells moved their static pea podders to our main yard at Nocton and Dunston station. At this time machinery began to improve, the estate bought some McBain pea cutters, which were mounted on the rear of the tractor, which had to be driven backwards when cutting the peas.

Also at this time, which was in the mid 50s, frozen peas were coming on the scene. The estate drew up a contract to join the Thimbleby Growers, growing peas for the Eskimo Company, who had a factory at Grimsby. The peas were all carted from the field to be vined at Thimbleby.

Late June, when the pea crop was ready, was the start of a very busy time. Peas had to be at the Grimsby Factory ready for the factory to start freezing at 8 am each morning. This meant that the field staff at Nocton had to start cutting and loading by 5 am to make sure the peas had been taken to Thimbleby and vined to arrive at Grimsby in time. We worked in the field 12 to 14 hours per day, seven days per week. We were gradually getting more mechanised in the field and had a green crop elevator loader in the field and also a Haypicker (we called it a back scratcher because you towed it

behind the lorry). And all the peas were moved up the Haypicker onto the rear of the lorry. With this tool you had to throw most of the peas forward by hand. It was an all weather job as the peas were soon past their ripening stage.

With the viners working continuously

P. Doughty fills the sprayer

at both Nocton and Thimbleby during the day, men had to be provided to wash down the viners during the night.

The next stage was the appearance of mobile viners. Our first ones were Scott Viners which were towed by a tractor and picked up the trail of vine after the pea cutter. As the peas were knocked out of the pods, they were collected on a rubber conveyor belt and deposited in a tank at the rear of the viner.

When the tank was full, it was hydraulically lifted and emptied into a trailer. The tanks were transferred into a lorry to be transported to the factory: either Morrells or Eskimos. There was always a time limit on each load: from pod to can or pod to freezing in four hours.

We then were equipped with seven Mather & Platt viners. These were bigger, with a larger output and we pulled them with Samme four-wheeldrive tractors or Muir Hills.

The next step was pea podders. These machines were self propelled and the peas

FMC Pea Podder, 1987 and Ford FW artic

didn't need cutting as the podders stripped the pea pods off the vine, leaving the vine still attached to the roots.

We also grew peas for Bachelors, which were marrow fat peas to be harvested dry for canning.

They grew on until they were almost dead before they were cut. Sometimes they were cut with the McBains and sometimes with a torpedo cutter. The torpedo cutter had large V blades, which cut the pea roots just under the ground. After the peas had dried and been turned a few times, tripods were erected in rows across the field. Then a gang of men would move in with hand forks and place the peas on the tripods. Piecework rate was 34/2d per acre, (£1.71].

After a week or two, when the peas were really dry, a threshing machine would be set up in the corner of the field and a tractor and buck rake were used to fetch the tripods of peas from the field to the threshing machine. This was the dirtiest job I ever took part in, especially when the peas were cut by the torpedo cutter. The amount of soil or dust created by the threshing operation was terrible. It really wasn't fit to be anywhere within the area. The amount of dust inhaled was tremendous. Piecework rate, by using seven men, plus elevator into stack instead of thresh-

Mr David Ellis, General Manager at Nocton until 1995

ing, was 9/- per acre per man (45p).

Cereals

Wheat was the main crop grown at Nocton during my working years. The yields have increased from about 1.25 tonne per acre to around 4.5 tonne in the aerly 21st century. The main reasons for this are better drainage, less weed competition (such as couch), more nitrogen, introduction of nutrients, mainly manganese on the organic soils, and also growth regulators that enable the crop to stand up to the weather without getting bashed to the floor. The experts would say fungicides and insecticides were one of the main reasons. In my opinion, they played their part but today thousands of gallons of spray are used unnecessarily, wasting thousands of pounds. Up to about the early 1990s, the crops were monitored more, thresholds of aphids had to be reached before it was cost effective to spray, and the same applied to diseases on cereals and other crops. Now it often seems that if the neighbour is out with his sprayer, then you should be. There might be an aphid in the field, or someone in the area might have found some yellow rust. Thousands of gallons of chemical are sprayed on just for protection, just in case the disease might come into the area.

In the 1950s and 60s, before the sprayer appeared on our farms, when the wheat crop had about four true leaves, and after the frosts had finished, the crop would be gang Cambridge rolled to consolidate the roots after they may have been lifted by the winter frosts. At this time at Nocton, the job would be done at piecework, 9d per acre (3.5p).

About a fortnight later the wheat crop would be harrowed: 1/- per acre (5p). The objective was to move any small weeds. The crop would then be left until harvest.

In the early 50s, when I started work, the sail reapers were getting towards the end of their working period: they were used only for cutting mustard seed. The Massy Harris, Deering, and Albion Binders, were then being used for cutting the cereals. As soon as the crop was ripe, two to four men (two mowing, two tying) would cut a strip around the crop so the horses or tractor pulling the binder could start cutting the crop without running over any. The piecework rate was 5/10 per acre (30p).

The crop would then be stooked at piecework rate of 13/4 per acre (67p).

When the crop had had time to ripen thoroughly in the stook, it would be carted and stacked either in the corner of the field or in the nearest farmyard. The piecework rate for a gang of six men, would be 8/5 (42p) per acre.

The next job was thatching, the thatch area was measured, by Eddie East from

Southery. The piecework rate paid to the thatchers was 9d per square yard (4p).

With the introduction of the combine harvester, all these jobs disappeared. In 1966 the minimum wage was £10.10/-. Piecework rates were almost finished with

J. Worrell drilling wheat, 1967

N. Woodhead drilling wheat, 1987

The power of the 1990s, John Deere, Ford and Massey Ferguson tractors

Wildlife on the Farm

The wildlife on the estate hadn't suffered much over the years up to 1995. This was mainly because of the staff and how they felt about it. Here are some examples. When cultivating for crops in the springtime most tractor drivers, on seeing a plovers nest, would stop and move the eggs, pull past the spot, remake the nest and put the eggs or young back again, and then mark the spot for any following drivers. Leverets would also be moved out of danger.

P. Cooke and M. Lovesey lift up the nest away from the high water level to Cone

5 Leverets

When the water was let into the fen dykes in the spring, any swan or moorhen's nests that were found were moved higher up the dyke banks.

Where possible, pheasants, partridges and ducks nests were marked with a stick or something. Probably the bird in most danger is the English partridge, mainly because of the disappearance of its food. These birds were most prominent on the high organic fen where the Willow weed or Pale Percicary grew, with better drainage and weeds being killed by spraying, they have almost disappeared. The barn owl had a tough time. The planners of today don't seem to plan for wildlife nesting sites, when passing new building plans. No ledges are made for nests and all buildings must be bird-proof. If each site was visited and assessed before plans were passed and locals were interviewed and asked such questions as, 'Were there any

A week or so later

barn owls, kestrels, swallows or bats seen or known to be nesting each year in the vicinity?' Very small and cheap alterations could be easily made to accommodate them. Ask any one that worked on or visited Nocton Fen over the last 20 years, 'Who saved the barn owl and kestrel in the fens?' They will say, 'Lenny Woodhead, with all his nest boxes.' Where possible, I used to put anything suitable such as old drums, lengths of pipes, and boxes in the top of any building I could. Over the last 15 to 20 years, we have had hatchings of barn owls, kestrels and tawny owls every year.

Said to be the first marsh harrier chicks to be hatched in Lincolnshire for 25 years, 1994

In 1994 the marsh harrier returned and nested in the fen, I was told this was the first time for 25 years. Four young ones flew from the nest and they are now returning each year. The main thing I think about from my time in the fens is who is going to look after the wildlife now? Money and progress seem to be more important to today's planners.

Young Mallards

The gamekeepers do a marvellous job. When they are feeding the pheasants and other games, they are also feeding the wild birds. You have only to visit Nocton woods about 3 o'clock on a winter's afternoon and look down the rides, where the gamekeeper has just scattered the food, to see the hundreds of small birds enjoying the feast. Gamekeepers also police the countryside: some poachers don't only come for the pheasants! The gamekeepers keep the rodent numbers down, ask any one in the Fen when they last saw a rat: they won't remember.

The skylark population has certainly gone down, and the water vole is down in numbers. I think probably the herons have eaten the voles. I've seen as many as 20 herons in the fen at one time, and I've seen them with voles in their beaks. I have also seen the marsh harriers catch them.

The house sparrow has suffered because of the disappearance of the old pantiled farm buildings, which have been replaced with corrugated asbestos, plastic or zinc. Their nesting sites have all gone, and any new pantiled roofs are made bird-proof.

When we first moved to Foxes Farm, in the late 1940s, and through the 50s, the Foxes and Langhams Drain were full of all sorts of wild life: snakes, frogs, and pike, up to 18 inches long. We used to spend hours with a snare made out of copper wire, walking along the banks of the two drains. We would snare the pike, and slip them quickly into a bucket of water to take them back home. In the middle of Foxes' yard was a large water tank. It held about 2000 gallons of water, and as it was fed by a spring it was always full. It had an over flow that went into Foxes' drain, this is where we used to put the pike. The most we had in it was 17.

In the late 50s, when the last horse had gone and the stackyard was to be stoned, the tank was getting the worse for wear and was in the way so it was decided that it should be scrapped. The pike were released back into the drains and the spring was re-routed into the Foxes' drain. A few years later, when the fields were being tile drained, most of the drains were gradually silting up with a thick yellow ochre, that was acid or low pH, which was being drawn into the drains from the newly drained fields. I think that probably this was the time when the fish based fertilisers were being replaced by the fertilisers that we use today. It all helped to pollute the waters and soon after came the chemicals or pesticides, these didn't help. Soon the water was empty of fish, frogs, snakes, and so on. Things seemed to improve again during the 70s and some wildlife returned but not the fish or snakes and frogs. They would be alright I think, but would have to be re-introduced. The main reason for the water improvement is the inflow during the summer months to enable the irrigation to operate. Other insects that have disappeared since I was a lad are grasshoppers. Every time we walked in the grass they would be jumping about. Where have they gone. They must be a casualty of the sprayer.

Nocton Estate Sick and Benefit Club

Committee   1950's

W.W. Watson (Chairman)
E.H.Turner (Secretary)

F.Woodhead, Section C, 16 Jubilee Street;
E.Cooke, Section C, Ruskington;
F.Redshaw,Heath, Sleaford, Lincs;

H.T.Brown (Treasurer)

Club Rules

1. Members shall be males of any age regularly employed on the estate, but casual employees shall not be included.
2. Any member shall be entitled to receive benefit the first week of membership.
3. Each member shall pay one shilling entrance fee in each year and one shilling per week contribution.
4. The benefit to be paid by this club in relief of sickness or accident shall be £1. 11. 0d per week for the first eight weeks and 16/- per week for the next eight weeks (work days only in one year). This completes benefit payable in any one year.
5. Should any member fall sick or meet with an accident he shall notify the secretary within three days, and send a copy of a doctor's certificate to the secretary in support of his claim. **To claim benefit members strictly adhere to this rule.**
6. If any member whilst on the club were

found intoxicated or from his own misconduct he shall not be entitled to any benefits from the club funds.
7. If any member depart this life each member shall contribute 2/- to the members widow or nearest of kin, to be deducted from each members share of the funds at the end of the year. In the event of the death of a second member each member shall be levied 2/-.
8. The funds in hand after deducting all expenses shall be divided at Christmas in each year.

The Washway

On the extreme east of Nocton Fen, next to the River Witham, there are about 100 acres of low land which are very high in organic content. We called this area the Washway. Over the 45 years I spent on the estate this land has changed dramatically. I first remember it as just an area of land covered with grass and reeds and most of the year partly covered with water. At that time it was fenced off and the heavy horses were put out at nights and weekends to graze it.

As time passed, with the horses leaving the farms and tractors coming in their place, the time had come to try to bring it into the farm-cropping programme. Small dykes were dug to try and get rid of the water. As the area was very wet, it was made into 20 fields anywhere from three to seven acres each. The small Caterpillar tractors such the 22 and D4s were sent in to plough. They had two-furrow trailer ploughs which took quite a lot of pulling, with it being so wet. Most of the growth was twitch, which was terrible stuff to go through the plough. The biggest problem of all was bog oaks. These were anywhere up to 40 ft in length and lying just below the black peaty soil. Each plough man or tractor driver carried a bundle of thatch pegs and when the plough struck one of the bog oaks, he would stop and stick in a peg to mark where it was. In the winter months, men and crawler tractors would spend weeks digging and pulling these big trees out of the fields.

Most times when a plough struck a bog oak it would break off the plough point so another would have to be fitted. Now we have quick release plough bodies so the bog oaks are not so troublesome. Subsoilers and most other implements are fitted with shear bolts. With better dykes and under drainage being done, the Washway has improved tremendously. The fields have also had thousands of tons of waste lime spread over them.

The Nocton Estate Staff 1961

Nocton Fen Section A
Foreman F Gash

Labourers	Fordson Tractors	Ferguson	Crawlers
J.B. Blackband	J.W. Blackband	C.S. Gash	H. Hodson
A. Rasen	J.H. Franklin	T. Hedison	
W.R. Jackson	P. Gash	R. Marshall	
J. Overton	B. Hewis	G.A. Robinson	
T. Overton			
A.T. Day	**Women**	**Allis Chalmers**	**International**
E. Sands	Mrs A.M. Carr	G.L. Gash	H. Freestone
C. Hewitt	Mrs D. Woodcock		F. Tomlinson
J. Woodcock			

Nocton Fen Section C
Foreman W Woodhead

Labourers	Fordson	Ferguson	Crawlers
A. Cooke	F. Stephenson	P. Chapman	L. Woodhead
E. Cooke	E. Joynes	R. Tomlinson	F. Pawlett
H. Goodyear	B. Woodhead	W.H. Tomlinson	R. Fox
S. Goodyear			
F. Woodhead	**Women**	**Nuffield**	
W. Page	Miss A. Page	B. Hewitt	
G.W. Tomlinson	Mrs E. Hewitt		

Middle Section

Foreman G Chambers

Labourers	Fordson	Ferguson	Crawlers
W.A. Franklin	M. Reek	K. Holden	A.F. Green
F. Jackson	G.W. Petch	K. Coxen	J. Fox
G. Redshaw	L. Massam	H. Robinson	
C.W. Turner	E. Redshaw	W. Elkington	**Allis Chalmers**
T. Jackson			B. Mitchell
H.E. Carter			
A. Melton			
E. Smith			

Dunston Fen Section

Foreman A Smith

Labourers	International	Ferguson	Crawlers
J.B. Flintham	R. Sellors	D. Sellors	G. Wakefield
T. Council	E. Sellars		
F. Stephenson	**Women**		
	Mrs K. Smith		

Heath Section

Foreman W Watson

Labourers	Fordson	Ferguson	Crawlers
T. Glossop	J.H. Worrel	J. Redding	A. Page
R. Pask	G. Ward	J. Kettleborough	
A. Franklin	A. Hardy	F.F. Doughty	
G. Baxter	B.L. Marr		
P. Ward	**Women**	**Allis Chalmers**	**International**
L. Marr	Mrs I. Baxter	K. Wilkinson	W. Franklin
C.E. Smith	Miss L. Castle		

25 years on Nocton Estate

On 28th March 1958, at a social gathering in Dunston Village Hall, with many employees present, Mr J. Ireson, the General Manager of the Smith's Potato Estate Nocton (Smith's Crisps), presented gold watches to 52 employees. All had worked for the company for 21 years, and been on the estate for 25 years or more. In January 1958, at the staff dinner, Mr Cyril J Scott, had presented seven others with gold watches.

The 52 were as follows:

F Bainbridge, J W Blackband, J Brumpton, W Carr, J H Chambers, T Council, A E Drage,
F Elvin, J B Flintham, W H Gash, H Goodyear, H Hodson, H Jackson, J W Ingall, J Kingswood, A Melton, W Redshaw, G Redshaw, F Sewell, A Smith, A Sleaford, W Tindall E H Turner, F Tye, B West, P Ward, J R Bird, H T Brown, M Brumpton, G T Chambers, A Cooke, E T Day, R Dykes, W H Fairweather, G H Gash, S Goodyear, C Hewitt, F Jackson, T Jackson, G R I'anson, T Melton, F Pawlett, E Redshaw, E J Sands, A Sleight, F Smith, J R Stephens,
E Towl, W D Turner, J R Wass, W Woodhead, J E Joung.

From this day onwards until 1995 any employee completing 25years service on the estate was presented with a gold watch Even though the estate had changed ownership several times.

Don Turner

Don was born at Dunston on 28th April 1911, his father kept the Dunston Post Office and delivered the mail. His grandfather was the village taylor. Don attended Dunston School. As he grew up he played football for Dunston United but his other great interest was cricket. He was one of the organisers of Nocton cricket club, and played for many years. When Don left school he started work on the Nocton Estate.

Apart from three years in the army, where he served in Northern Ireland, Italy, and Palestine, he devoted his time to the estate and village life.

At home in Nocton he was in the Home Guard, during his time on the estate he was Miller, Lorry Driver, Transport Manager, in the days of the Nocton Light Railway, and for many years in charge of the estate corn dryers.

When he got married in the early 1930s, he and his new wife, Nell, set up house in the Old Row at Nocton. This was when he first got involved in the social life of the village.

He joined the Cricket Club, the Estate Sports Club, the Social Club, from its beginning, and he was also on the Village Hall Management committee, the Parochial Church Council, and later the Friendship Club. Right up to his death he was MC at all the Whist Drives. During his time as MC, almost £4000 was made for the Friendship Club.

In 1977, Don was awarded the Queen's Jubilee Medal for his service to the Community.

In 1958 he was one of over 50 estate workers who received a gold watch for 21 years service. In this era people spent their whole life in the villages and made their own entertainment.

It just needed a few like Don to organise things. The passing on of these great village characters, such as Don, leaves those of us who knew him thankful and proud that we were part of the village scene at that time.

FMC Pea Podder, 1987

Getting it back on its wheels

An easy way to empty a load of beet

No more harvest today, 1995

Beware of icy roads, 1986

A Few Important Dates

1.4.48	Total horses on the estate =154.
1.1.48	Total sheep on the estate =1350.
29.12.55	Total cattle on the estate = 968.
11.5.61	Dairy cattle left the estate on this date.
10.2.66	The poultry left on this date.
8.5.69	Last cattle left on this date.
11.4.68	Last horse left on this date.
21.10.71	Finished making pig rations at the mill at railhead on this date.

The Changes and Modernisation of Nocton

The old Tenrow houses were altered over the years to make them larger. This was done by making two houses into one. In 1983, the row was bought by Simons builders, stripped and modernised. When they were finished the houses were sold off and are as you see them today. After modernisation, they sold for around £24,000 each, in 1989.

Halls yard originally consisted of a farmhouse and a large barn, used in the past for fertiliser storage. Later it was used as a chitting house for seed potatoes. More recently the barn has been converted into a house. There were five garages used by the estate foremen for their vehicles, these have now been made into a bungalow. At the other end of the yard was a large open waggon oval. This has been converted into a garage for Mr J Watt, who has also built a house in the yard. In the opposite corner of the yard is a bungalow, which was made out of some old stables and the crewyard. This was done in the 50s to accommodate some poultry girls.

There were two other areas facing south which used to be stables and crewyards, one next to the manor house garden has been converted into a bungalow; the other one, which a few years ago was a shed for large tractors, is now part of the gardens and garage of the converted barn.

A view of the converted garages Halls yard. 2000

Shephard's bungalow next to Manor Halls Yard Crew Yard before being converted

Halls barn with garages in the background, and where the excavator stands there now stands a large house

Shephard's bungalow

Halls barn from the south / tractor sheds

Halls barn from the south converted

Wrays yard buildings consisted of the large buildings on the right hand side. In the 40s, these were a partly open crewyard used for horses and bullocks, with stables at the rear. Later the fronts were bricked up and the large parts were used for chitting seed potatoes, after that they were used as tractor sheds. Now they are two lovely bungalows. As you walk into the yard, looking straight ahead is the old barn, this was used for storing fertiliser and then later made into a seed potato chitting house. In the rear of the yard were further crewyards for bullocks and pigs. Some fine houses have now been built here.

Wrays tractor shed or crewyard, 1993

The large buildings on the right of Wrays yard

The above building after conversion into a bungalow

The second part of the building after conversion

Wrays barn being converted into a bungalow

The manor yard had a large dairy herd when I was a lad at Nocton School. It was quite an impressive farmyard at that time, the 40s and 50s. There was a T.T. tested dairy herd and during the 50s some new bull pens were built, but on the 11th May 1961 the last of the herd was sold.

After this date the crewyards were used for fattening bullocks and, for many years, all the lambing was done there. It has now been sold off to a developer to build ten houses. One or more of the old buildings were to be kept and made into houses in order to keep a little bit of the old character, but something went wrong and the whole site was demolished and cleared.

The old chitting house or barn, Wrays yard, 1993

The manor yard from the Southwest corner, with bull pens in the background

The manor yard taken from a similar position today

The manor yard from the east, 1990

The manor yard from the south, 1990

Taken from a similar position, 2000

The old post office under re-construction by Mr Swinbourn, 1987

The old post office after re-construction

On Burns Night, 1979, the Nocton Village Hall and Social CLub burnt to the ground

Out of the ashes a new village hall was builtt

Mr Hargreaves, our new licensee, declares our new social club open

Mr D. Turner, our retiring secretary, pulls the first pint in our new club room

Right: A group of thirsty club members: Hemmings, Hardy, Hewitt, Woodhead, Russel, Pygot and others

Thoughts for the Future

The farming community is in trouble at the moment. The sheep and beef herds are the lawn mowers of the countryside and I see no future for hill farmers or dairy farmers unless they can get more help from the government. Just imagine riding through Yorkshire, Derbyshire or the lovely hills of Wales, what would it be like after five or six years with fewer sheep and cattle grazing? You have only to take a walk along the river banks, such as the River Witham banks from Bardney southwards towards Boston. These used to be grazed by the cattle or sheep of local farmers. Now all you see are perennial plants such as thistles, nettles, hemlock and such like. These make access difficult and also, like bracken on the Yorkshire moors, smother out almost all the meadow growing flowers, such as daisy's, dandelions, buttercups, clovers, and many more.

Who will look after the countryside in a future like that? What will the public footpaths be like on the hills and moors of our Midland Counties? The farmers of the present day are expected to keep all these clear for hardly any reward. What would the ramblers and walkers say then? What a task for any new department to take on! It's a fact those who enjoy the countryside wouldn't be looked after like they are now. We wouldn't be walking hills and moors free of charge. We, as tax payers or council tax payers, would be paying for something the farmer is now doing for almost nothing.

Our sheep and dairy farmers need immediate help now to look after our countryside: in a few years most of them will be gone, to the detriment of us all. The government and also the supermarkets who are, with their monopoly, making slaves out of our smaller British farmers need to plan for the future.

It's a pity that there isn't a way to turn the tables around, with some farming body buying out one of the larger supermarkets.

Arable farming will survive but farmers must be given a level playing field with our so-called European partners.

Our animal farmers have not had this benefit to their detriment.

What changes in agriculture shall we see by 2100? During the last 100 years we have seen tremendous changes, from manual work being replaced by mechanical, and now even controlled by computers, where could we go from here?

We seem to have had a similar period, during the 1970s, to what we are experiencing now: about the time we first got involved with Europe. For several years we seemed to be held back in modernising our implements and tractors. I think this was to allow our new European partners to catch up. I can see this happening again shortly if and when we extend the European membership to more eastern European Countries. We, as a hard-working rural farming industry will be held back whilst millions of £s of our money is pumped into the new eastern member states. Then as we are now, we shall be the only member that obeys the rules drawn up by overpaid unelected people that know very little about the countryside struggling to produce cheap food with the odds still stacked against us.

We shall also, during this century, be running short of fossil fuels. I predict that the next step will be electric steam engines. I would have thought that with the expertise available today, water could be heated by electricity from batteries therefore producing steam to drive an engine and, at the same time, generating enough extra voltage to keep the batteries charged.

And of course we could use wind and wave power for our national grid.

The Stars

I think, within the next 50 years, we will find other planets in the universe with life on. Think of when Captain Cook set sail and the discoveries he made, also Columbus. The secrets of the sea at that time were just as great as the enormous space above us today. How many people at that time thought of other islands or countries with people living in them?

GM Crops

What are we doing now to cause problems for the future? Glyphosate (Roundup): plants such as rape, sugar beet, and maize, are being developed to withstand this chemical. In a few years time the countryside will be over grown with oilseed rape and wild beet, which is already a problem. If these developments are a success, the whole crop would sprayed with Glyphosate, killing everything except these genetically modified plants. Wild beet would grow rampant everywhere, and rape would be a bigger problem, being an oil seed, it would lay dormant longer in the soil.

We already have a beet cross pollinated with fat hen growing happily on the lower part of the fens, and on the Bardney Sugar filter beds. But I think the main GM worry is when animal and human genes are injected into plants, as we are now beginning to hear about.

Why do we need to increase yields? There's a surplus of wheat, barley, sugar, and oil seeds.

If we need to increase yields to feed the hungry in Africa and other poor countries, why do we set aside the best productive farming land in England, and then spend thousands of £'s on GM trials to produce more when we can so easily produce more without GM.

As I write, a proposal comes through from the EU saying that they are thinking of letting five million tons of sugar into the EEC from the rest of the world. Imagine what this will do, we only produce 12 million tons in the EEC at the present time so there goes hundreds of acres of good farming land. What can we grow in its place and how many sugar factories will close? By losing 40% of the sugar tonnage?, how many more farmers will go out of business?

Bardney sugar factory was built in 1928. Today is the 24th January 2001. It has just been announced on the news that Bardney, Ipswich and Kidderminster factories are to close for good in February. This means we are loosing our last sugar factory in Lincolnshire, which I would think is most likely the largest beet growing county in England, so the 900,000 tonne of beet processed at Bardney annually is now to be hauled to Newark. I would think that total will shrink as many small farmers will not be able to grow at a profitable rate to cover the hire of a lorry, instead of being able to use his old tractor and trailer. Why are we limited by the EEC to grow only 51% of the sugar our country needs".

In the 1970s thousands of £s were invested by our arable farmers to build reservoirs to irrigate the land and produce more potatoes, etc. In most cases this increased the potato yield from around 12 tonnes per acre to around 18 to 20 tonne, then down comes the price to the farmer, so all the money invested is lost. If we had stayed as we were, we needn't have had set-aside. So are GM crops needed?

The EEC

Yes, there will be a referendum for joining the euro. The question will be in some gobbledegook phrase so the country will not know clearly how to vote, or we will be told that the three conditions are perfect, not really knowing what the conditions are.

So we shall join, but I think we will draw out of the EEC by 2010.

If it is so important to be in a United States of Europe, and loose our English identity, then why are Scotland and Wales so keen for self government, breaking up a united British Isles.

The question we should be asked is: in a democracy why should our country be ruled or (ruined) by decisions made by unselected Commissioners, or people that were rejected by the people of Britain in the first place? Democratic candidates voted in by the people of the country they represent should fill all decision-making posts, not those elected by friends in higher places.

Memories that Stick in my Mind

After about three hours lifting up heavy wheat sheaves out of stooks in harvest time and sitting down at a stook for tea. Someone would have brought a lovely can of hot tea from the nearest farm house, down the farm road would often come Jim Clift's Bakers van from Bardney, with lovely new bread that may have been taken out of the oven about 15 minutes

earlier. The van would also bring fresh cream buns, still warm from the bakehouse. There was nothing better than home-grown tomatoes, and a slice of new bread with the butter melting in the sandwich.

When I first started work I used to lie in bed in the morning until Mum had lit the fire. I could hear the fire roaring up the chimney from our bedroom, and the bedrooms were very cold. In winter, the windows would have large ice patterns on the inside. I used to nip down stairs and sit near the fire to put my boots on.

I remember Mum's hot rice pudding with a lovely sweet skin on top. We could eat puddings then and we never got fat.

Coming home at night to a lovely hot meal after sitting out on a tractor all day, without a cab on the tractor, in the middle of winter was very comforting. You had to keep going in most weather situations, with all work done on a piecework rate: no work, no money.

Again coming home at night in the middle of winter after being stood for eight hours outside, picking off a potato riddle, I would be so cold I couldn't feel my hands or feet.

Getting off a combine harvester at 11o'clock at night, after being sat there all day with no cab, cutting barley, was a great relief. My eye's would be sore with barley horns.

After a long day ploughing down the bottom of Nocton Fen, I enjoyed jumping on my bike and peddaling all the way home to Nocton. There always seemed to be headwind. Finally opening the house door, seeing a nice fire, a lovely wife and two kids: this was heaven.

Jumping on my bike to go home after a days bush beating, when it had been a hare shoot was memorable. After walking across ploughed fields all day, maybe carrying a couple of hares, our boots would be carrying pounds of extra weight, our legs felt as if they were going to drop off.

Going out on a bright May morning, about 6 am, and hearing the skylarks singing from their positions way up in the sky: sitting down on a dyke bank to have my dinner, listening to the grasshoppers, and seeing them jumping about in the grass. These are happy memories.

When picking potatoes you had just finished picking your length of row, and then, with your back aching like fury, you would straighten up and the b.... spinner would be coming down again.

Here is a story to remember. A gang of about 12 Irishmen were planting potatoes by hand down the bottom of Potterhanworth Fen. At the north end of the field, over the dyke from where they were working stood a cottage. Standing in the garden was the gentleman who lived there. On one part of the garden he had put a stick, as the men came to the end of the field, he shouted, 'hey you lot, I bet you can't hit that stick.' They soon started throwing seed potatoes, after throwing for some time, the old chap shouted for them to give up. It seemed they had thrown enough to plant his garden.

I think it was 1947, but anyway the snow had fallen heavily for a few days, and we had several inches. We were short of water and there was no way the loco was going to get down the fen for a few days to bring us any. My mother set off across TD8 which was about a quarter of a mile to the Nocton Delf, with two empty buckets, After having quite a job to break the ice, she returned later with her buckets full of water. She had to boil the water before she could use it to cook with. (They don't make them like that any more!) One other thing she did several times was collect some snow and let it melt, for use in the house.

I remember one cold and frosty morning, it was very foggy, and there was hard packed snow or ice on the roads. I, along with another work mate, had managed to get a lift in an old Ford van. I think the driver was a contract worker who was working for Richmonds drainage.

We were going down Foxes farm road to the large greenhouse for our lunch. There was a deep ditch on our right and a fair drop off the road on our left, into the field. At that time most cars and vans were equipped with only six volt batteries. As we travelled along the road, the snow came down heavily and was collecting on the windscreen. We were getting a bit uncomfortable as the van was sliding about quite a bit, and we didn't like the look of the large ditch. I said to the driver, 'why don't you put your windscreen wipers on?' We could hardly see where we were going. He said, 'I can't do that mate it'll ruin me battery.' He got a bit further down the road and we couldn't see at all. He had to switch the wipers on but, by then, they were frozen to the glass, so when he flicked the switch the wiper arm broke. We have often talked about thus event, it seemed funny at the time, although it was dangerous.

On the way home from Bardney school one day, I saw in the Post Office window a note saying, White Mice For Sale. After asking about these in the shop, I was told by Mrs Chapman that Barry and Brenda, their children, kept these mice and they were getting quite a large number so they had decided to sell some of them.

I was told that a large doe would cost 2d. The mouse was put in a small box and I paid my 2d. I went outside and caught Hudsons bus to take me the three miles home. I hadn't gone far on the bus before every one sitting nearby was moving further away from me, and then I realized how much the mouse smelled. What everyone thought, I shall never know, because I don't think anyone knew I had a mouse in my pocket, I suppose they thought it was me.

I soon realized why the mouse was fat, within a day or so I had a cage full of baby mice.

Fen Dialect

They wos foore boort lourd of em,
He went like ell round corna strate in the
dake,
I nivver herd im commin thru the dooer,
He must a bin out becos ee wont in is cre-
ers,
Pick that bag a tates up an put it on the
loored then tekit an put it i the shed,
He wos soor laert comin hoorm las night
id bin drinkin moorst o the dayer,
I nivver sor im comin he it that oorl in the
roord an brok is weel off is moorter,
I wos laret up agearn this mornin soer
idint git mi barecon an eggs,
Na mayert it's a funny ode mornin is it
gooin to raren du ya rekon,
   Nar mairt ow a ya this mornin or not
sa bad, but a had sum bad noos this morning, ode jak up tha roord dide but mine ya
he wos nearly aty, it woris mi a bit dunt it
yoo, it alast remins mi o me ode grand-
dad, e wos a bit of a shepad ya nor,e said
ta me won morning, na mi lad yar or rate-
until he starts tekin out a yoor pen, its
gitin a bit close nar.

   Ode Jack was called round nex door.
The ode wuman sed the privy pipe wos
bunged up, edy got any rods or ote ta un
bugit, soor Jack went ta eva look, he soon
ed it gooin agen. When id dun he wnt ta
the house an nokt opn the door. The ode
lady cum to the door an sed aja dun it
Jack, e ses yis I ev, ya nor wots the matta
doont ya, she ses noor idoont, wel al telya
the trouble is ya s*≠ • a four inch turd in
a three inch pipe.

Notes

Notes

Notes